THE
REAL TRUTH
ABOUT
CHURCH
HISTORY

JAMES SHARP

Copyright © 2022 James Sharp.

All rights reserved. No part of this book may be reproduced, stored, or transmitted by any means—whether auditory, graphic, mechanical, or electronic—without written permission of both publisher and author, except in the case of brief excerpts used in critical articles and reviews. Unauthorized reproduction of any part of this work is illegal and is punishable by law.

Scripture quotations marked (KJV) are taken from the *Holy Bible, King James Version*, Cambridge, 1769. Used by permission. All rights reserved.

Scripture quotations marked (NASB) are taken from the *New American Standard Bible®*, Copyright © 1960, 1962, 1963, 1968, 1971, 1972, 1973, 1975, 1977, 1995 by The Lockman Foundation. Used by permission.

Scripture quotations marked (NIV) are taken from the *Holy Bible, New International Version®*, niv®. Copyright © 1973, 1978, 1984 by Biblica, Inc.™ Used by permission of Zondervan. All rights reserved worldwide. www.zondervan.com

Scripture quotations marked (NKJV) are taken from the *New King James Version*. Copyright © 1982 by Thomas Nelson, Inc. Used by permission. All rights reserved.

Scripture quotations marked (NLT) are taken from the *Holy Bible, New Living Translation*, copyright © 1996. Used by permission of Tyndale House Publishers, Inc., Wheaton, Illinois 60189. All rights reserved.

ISBN: 979-8-88640-737-2 (sc)
ISBN: 979-8-88640-738-9 (hc)
ISBN: 979-8-88640-739-6 (e)

Because of the dynamic nature of the Internet, any web addresses or links contained in this book may have changed since publication and may no longer be valid. The views expressed in this work are solely those of the author and do not necessarily reflect the views of the publisher, and the publisher hereby disclaims any responsibility for them.

One Galleria Blvd., Suite 1900, Metairie, LA 70001
1-888-421-2397

And I say also unto thee, That thou art Peter, and upon this rock I will build my church; and the gates of hell shall not prevail against it. (Matt. 16:18)

This book is dedicated to my Lord and Savior, Jesus Christ, the God of truth made known in the flesh. Also, I dedicate this book to all the saints of God who have worked tirelessly to research the truth about church history. Because of your efforts and with God leading me to your works online, this book exists. I've acknowledged all of you precious saints throughout this book. I thank all of you, great writers, researchers, and church historians that are members of the household of faith. Again, I say, thank you. May our God Jesus bless all of you with favor in the areas of your life where it is needed most. Lastly, this book is dedicated to all the saints of God worldwide. Since God is one, let us all be one in Christ, even though many of us are far apart. For Christ is all and in us all.

CONTENTS

Author's Preface ix

Introduction xi

Chapter 1 The First Century, Part 1 1

Chapter 2 The First Century, Part 2 34

Chapter 3 The Second Century 64

Chapter 4 The Third Century 92

Chapter 5 The Fourth Century 118

Chapter 6 The Fifth Century 145

Appendix: Timeline 169

Bibliography 187

AUTHOR'S PREFACE

This book is volume one of a series in church history. The present volume covers the first five centuries of the church age. Also, this volume covers important historical events that were happening outside of God's messianic community. The first two chapters of this book talk about the first century. It took two chapters to cover the first century because so many things happened during this period. God inspired the New Testament, and He, through His church, accomplished so many things to lay the foundation of primitive Christian theology. Chapter three covers what God had accomplished through His church in the second century. It also covers the emergence of the ancient Catholic Church. The remaining chapters talk about what God had accomplished through His church in the third, fourth, and fifth centuries. They also cover very important historical events that influenced Catholicism, brought about the fall of the Roman Empire, and brought about the Dark Ages in Western Europe. In addition, this series consists of four volumes. Each volume will cover five centuries at a time. As of this writing, volume 2, which will cover the sixth to the tenth centuries, is still in the planning and research stage. My goal is to write volumes two, three, and four. The fourth volume will end with the twenty-first century.

The purpose of this book is to tell the truth about the New Testament and church history. Now let me state the facts: I'm telling you the exact same story that all of us have been told in school or college. I did this because what happened in the past actually happened. So in addition to telling you the exact same story, I brought out the facts about God's primitive church more clearly. The church of the New Testament is one hundred years older than the Roman Catholic Church, and my book proves this fact to be true. I've got the references to back up my claims, and they can be found in this book's bibliography. I know that I'm making bold statements, but I'm coming boldly in the name of the Lord Jesus Christ!

Please be advised that this book uses several different versions of the Holy Bible. These versions include the following: The King James Version, New King James Version, New International Version, New American Standard Bible, The New Living Translation, and the JPS Bible. Also, I used the Complete Jewish Bible to help me write this book as well.

INTRODUCTION

I was saved by the Lord Jesus Christ on Monday, December 20, 2004. That was the greatest day of my life because I stopped fearing death itself. There is nothing like being born again of the water and of the Spirit. But after a month of being saved, I noticed something about the Christian world. I questioned, why are there so many Christian denominations? And why does each Christian denomination teach a doctrine that is different from another denomination? As a result of this fact, I didn't know which church I should attend. I say this because I didn't know much about the Christian world before I got saved. And I thought that all churches preached and taught the same thing.

The church that I got saved at showed me the Scriptures in the Holy Bible that teaches the church how a sinner gets saved. So I knew that my salvation was biblical because I was there when God gave me the Holy Spirit. But I remembered the days when I was attending a Baptist church in the mid-nineties. What that church taught was different from the church where God had saved me. Then I thought about the other Christian denominations that still exist till this day. I had a severe problem with the fact that there are some many differences of opinion in the Christian world. So I didn't trust any pastor, including the pastor of the church where God had saved me.

Toward the end of January 2005, I prayed a prayer to the Lord. I asked Him specifically to prove to me through church history that He really had a church, and I needed Him to show me that He sustained it and its doctrine all throughout the centuries. Also, I asked God to show me what the original church taught, and I needed Him to show me that what the original church preached and taught never changed from the first century to today. Lastly, I told God that if He does this for me, then I promised to stay in His church till the end. This was the only way that I could be sure that God really established a church that had and has never changed. I never questioned my salvation, but I needed to understand why the doctrines of the twenty-first century church world are so different from that of the first century church.

I didn't know it at that time, but faith in God without works is dead. So after I prayed, I humbled myself and went off to research church history. I was blessed because I worked at the California State Dominguez Hills University Library throughout my undergraduate years as a Student Assistant. I worked at the librarian's desk, and my job taught me how to research and find books for other students. So I conducted my research there, and I did my research on the Internet as well.

From January to November 2005, I found and read the best of the best encyclopedias and Bible dictionaries. Then I researched and found the best of the best online resources. My research focused on three things: (1) the history of the Roman Catholic Church, (2) the history of the book of Acts, and (3) the history of the New Testament form of salvation from the first century to today. What God showed me was astounding. For example, Catholic scholar H. Mueller wrote the following in the New Catholic Encyclopedia, volume 2: "The NT defines neither the exact rite of Baptism nor the exact formulas." Mueller is talking about the New Testament. How can the Holy Bible be the infallible and inspired Word of God, but it can't tell me how to be properly baptized? In fact, this same article on baptism, in its own words, states that the New Testament does not define the exact formula of baptism three more times! This is the Roman Catholic Church, which is supposed to be the oldest Christian denomination in the world!

After I read Mueller's statement, I knew that there was something wrong with many of the thoughts and teachings of the Catholic Church.

God did something else for me while I was researching church history. He showed me that the New Testament church of the first century never changed in the second century, third century, fourth century, and each and every century till the twenty-first century. In fact, God showed me that the first century church is older than the Roman Catholic Church. At first, this was hard to believe. But as I kept on researching, it was impossible to deny the documented fact that the Catholic Church is an independent church that got started in the second century. The New Testament church never turned into the Catholic Church, and the Catholic Church was and still is something completely different from the church of the first century. In addition, God dealt with me to let me know that He wanted me to attend the church where I had embraced the gospel of Jesus Christ. So I obeyed Him and attended that church. I'm still at my church home this very day.

After I finished my research, everything about church history was clear to me. Now I understand how and why the Catholic Church came on the scene in the second century. I understand why it became so powerful and is so different from the New Testament church. Also, I understand why the Protestant Reformation happened in the first place. And I understand why mainstream Christianity is what it is today. God still has a church. But from the twentieth century to the twenty-first century, the Christian world has gone completely downhill. And there's much work to be done to fix it.

When I concluded my research, I had over a thousand pages of documented facts about church history. That may not sound like much, but I was able to condense my research because of the Internet. I had all this information at my disposal. At first, I thought that God had given this information to me for my benefit alone. Also, I thought that there was no need for me to share it with the world by writing a book or something of the like. Plus, I knew that I wasn't the only one who knew what I know about church history. But I knew that there's only a small percentage of people in this world that are saved and know the truth about church history. And I had become one of them. So I had no intentions of writing a book at all. But in the spring of 2006, God began to deal with me.

The first thing I did was read the New Testament from start to finish. I finished reading the New Testament in the summer of 2006. Then, in the next two years, God kept dealing with me about writing a book about my research. So in 2008, I finally gave in and agreed with God to write this book. But before I could get started, the Lord let me know that He wanted me to read the Old Testament. The Lord Jesus literally gave me a hunger to read the Old Testament. And when I began to read it, I couldn't put it down. So after many months, I finished reading the Old Testament in the autumn of 2008.

I have researched and tried the Holy Bible for myself. I know that it is the infallible and inspired word of God, and I know what it says for myself. I am a Bible-believing Christian who has read the entire Bible, including the book of Revelations, eleven times. Also, I can say with confidence that Jesus Christ is Lord and God. The Lord answered my prayer, and I'm still upholding my end of the bargain by staying in the faith that God had delivered unto me.

My mission is to educate the whole world about primitive Christianity and church history one person at a time. I'm telling the exact same story of church history that a lot of us have been told. But the facts that have been hidden have been brought out more clearly by me. These facts have been documented, and they cannot be refuted. And I know that you will enjoy my work, regardless of your Christian denomination. The truth is shining brighter than the noonday sun, and it is time for the lies and deception to end now! So enjoy the ride! And may all the saints of God come together as one, just like the first century church.

THE FIRST CENTURY, PART 1

The year is AD 30. Jesus Christ fulfilled all the Old Testament prophecies concerning the first coming of the Anointed One by suffering severe torture, dying a brutal death on a cross, and being buried in a tomb. But on the third day of His death, by the power of God the Father, the Messiah Jesus resurrected Himself from the dead. The Lord Jesus did this in order to become the captain of our salvation, made perfect through shedding His blood, so that He could save the world from our sins. Once our captain was glorified, He dwelt with His disciples for forty days and showed proof to them that He is alive! Before Jesus Christ ascended back into heaven, He commanded His disciples to go to Jerusalem and stay there. Also, Jesus said, "For John truly baptized with water; but you shall be baptized with the Holy Ghost not many days hence" (Acts 1:5, King James Version). After He said these encouraging words to them, Jesus ascended into heaven. Then the followers of Jesus, after seeing Him go up into heaven, went to Jerusalem with great joy! They entered into an upper room where they were staying. Altogether, there were about 120 people staying in that upper room. There were only eleven disciples because Judas Iscariot, the one who betrayed Jesus, hanged himself. While in that upper room,

Simon Peter and the other disciples prayed to the Lord Jesus so that the Lord would reveal to them who will take part in the apostolic ministry with the original eleven. After they finished praying, they cast lots between Barsabas and Matthias. The lot that they cast fell on Matthias; he would become the twelfth apostle until God would call and save Saul of Tarsus, also known as Paul.

The Day of Pentecost occurred fifty days after the resurrection of Jesus the Messiah. On this day, the 120 people were all together in one place. And there came suddenly a sound out of heaven as of a violent blowing wind, and it filled the whole house where they were sitting. They were all filled with the Holy Ghost and began to speak with other tongues as the Spirit empowered them to speak. While this was happening, all the God-fearing Jews from the nations located in ancient Africa, Asia, and Europe were staying in Jerusalem to observe the Feast of Pentecost, which occurs fifty days after the first Sunday of the Feast of Unleavened Bread. By the way, the number fifty means time of great joy or deliverance. Also, this number points to deliverance and rest following on as the result of the perfect consummation of time. The prophet Isaiah said, "This is the resting place, let the weary rest; this is the place of repose" (Isa. 28:12, JPS Bible). The Bible calls the Holy Ghost the rest and the refreshing. So when the proper time came, God poured out His Spirit just as the prophet John the Baptizer had predicted. Now let's get back to the story.

THE BEGINNING OF THE CHURCH

The sound of the 120 people speaking in various languages came to the Jews who were staying in Jerusalem near that upper room. A crowd of them went to the upper room, and they saw and heard the disciples of Jesus speaking in their own languages and declaring the wonders of God. These Jews were amazed because the disciples were Galileans who only spoke two languages: Aramaic and Greek.

Some of the Jews asked one another, "What does this mean?"

But others made fun of the disciples for speaking in tongues and said that they were drunk from drinking too much wine.

Then Peter boldly stood up with the original eleven and explained to the Jews that not only are the disciples not drunk, but they are seeing the fulfillment of the prophet Joel's prophecy right before their eyes. Peter quoted Joel by saying, "And it shall come to pass in the last days, saith God, I will pour out of My Spirit upon all flesh" (Acts 2:17, KJV) . Peter preached a long sermon to the Jews concerning the death, burial, and resurrection of Jesus Christ. With many words, Peter explained to the Jews that Jesus is the Messiah and that they, through wicked men, put Him to death on a cross. But God raised Him from the dead and placed Him at the highest position in heaven. And through the Lord Jesus the Messiah, God has poured out the Holy Ghost, which the Jews saw and heard. Then Peter reiterated to the Jews that Jesus, the One they crucified, is both Lord and the Messiah. The words of Peter stabbed the Jews in the heart!

The Jews asked the disciples what they should do about their current predicament. Peter gave them the answer by saying, "Each of you must repent of your sins and turn to God, and be baptized in the name of Jesus Christ for the forgiveness of your sins. Then you will receive the gift of the Holy Spirit" (Acts 2:38, New Living Translation). Peter told them to do this because this constitutes the New Birth! After he told the Jews what to do, Peter spoke many words to them and pleaded with them to save themselves. And those who gladly received Peter's message agreed to be baptized. So the apostles and disciples of Christ, including those Jews, went to a place where there was much water. Then all of them were baptized in the name of Jesus the Messiah. And those Jews who didn't already have the Holy Ghost were baptized with the Holy Ghost and fire by the Lord Jesus. About 3,120 souls were saved on that great day! So the dispensation of grace (the church age) began in the Roman Empire, during the reign of Emperor Tiberius (AD 14–37).

The new converts continually devoted themselves to the apostle's doctrine, and the Lord Jesus continued to save sinners every day. The visitors to Jerusalem who were saved carried the apostle's doctrine back to their home lands. The Spirit of God blessed His saints with favor with all people, and God used His saints to witness to different people and save them. God also performed many kinds of wonders and miracles through His emissaries to prove to the people that the apostles are men of God. Peter continued to preach that Jesus is the Son of God. In fact, Peter and the apostle John preached Jesus so much that the priests, the Sadducees, and the captain of the temple guard put them in jail overnight to silence them. But many who heard their message believed in Jesus, and another Holy Ghost outpouring occurred. The number of people who heard the message of salvation and believed grew to about five thousand. The Holy Ghost was just falling like rain on these Jews!

On the next day, the rulers and the teachers of the Torah (the Law) had Peter and John brought before them and began to question them. They asked them, "By what power or what name did you do this?" This question was concerning Peter healing a crippled man. Peter answered them, "It is by the name of Jesus Christ of Nazareth, whom you crucified but whom God raised from the dead, that this man stands before you healed" (Acts 4:10, New International Version). Then Peter said to them, "And there is salvation in no one else; for there is no other Name under Heaven that has been given among men, by which we must be saved" (Acts 4:12, New American Standard Bible). Shortly after Peter said these things to them, the Sanhedrin commanded and threatened them to stop preaching and teaching in the name of Jesus. Peter and John went back to their messianic communities and told them what had happened to them. Because of the threats of the Sanhedrin, they prayed to the Lord Jesus, asking Him to enable the saints to speak the word of God with boldness. After they finished praying, the place where they had prayed was shaken. And God strengthened them through the power of the Holy Ghost to boldly speak the word of God.

The churches were one in heart and mind. In other words, they had everything in common. The disciples of Christ spoke the word of God boldly, and the Lord Jesus added new souls to His church daily. The apostles performed miracles in front of the Jews. Also, they healed many people and had cast demonic spirits (fallen angels) out of those who were possessed and tormented by them. These things were happening on a daily basis. Some of the members of the Sanhedrin saw what was happening, and they became jealous of the apostles. That's right, jealous! As a result of their jealously, they put the apostles in a public jail. This marks the beginning of the persecution of the saints, and it would only get worse. But persecution could not stop the apostles from proclaiming the name of Jesus.

For example, while the apostles were in jail, an angel from God opened the gates of the prison and told the apostles to go their way and continue to speak to the people the message of this new life. At daybreak, they entered the temple courts and did everything that the angel had told them to do. Yes, world, this actually happened. The Sanhedrin sent for the apostles so that they could be questioned by the Jewish high priest. When they arrived at the public jail, they saw that the apostles were gone. They were deeply troubled about this, and they wondered what would happen because of this. Then someone noticed that the apostles were teaching the people on the temple courts.

The apostles were brought to the Sanhedrin, and the high priest said, "We gave you strict orders not to teach in this Name" (Acts 5:28, niv). He was concerned because the apostles had filled Jerusalem with the message of the good news of Jesus the Messiah. The high priest thought that they were determined to make them guilty of killing Jesus.

Peter replied by telling the Sanhedrin that they would rather obey God than men. Also, Peter said, "The God of our fathers raised up Jesus, whom you slew and hanged on a tree. Him has God exalted with His right hand to be a Prince and a Savior, for to give repentance to Israel, and forgiveness of sins. And we are His witnesses of these things; and so is also the Holy Ghost, whom God has given to them that obey Him" (Acts 5:30–32, KJV). In order to receive the gift of the Holy Ghost, you must obey God by repenting of your sins.

When the Sanhedrin heard this, they wanted to kill the apostles. But Gamaliel, a teacher of the law, persuaded the members of the Sanhedrin not to kill the apostles. He said, "Let them go! For if their purpose or activity is of human origin, it will fail. But if it is from God, you will not be able to stop these men; you will only find yourselves fighting against God" (Acts 5:38–39, NIV). After Gamaliel said these words to the Sanhedrin, they flogged the apostles. In other words, the emissaries were severely whipped. Before they released the apostles, the Sanhedrin ordered them to stop speaking and teaching about *Yeshua* (Jesus).

After the apostles left the Sanhedrin, they rejoiced because they were counted worthy to suffer shame for the name of Jesus. And day after day, the apostles never stopped teaching and proclaiming to the people that Jesus is the Messiah. Now the world would consider the apostles to be crazy. But to those of us who are in the Spirit, we know that they rejoiced because when they were put to the test, they maintained their faith and integrity before the Sanhedrin. And shortly after the rapture of the church, the Lord Jesus will give them a crown of life for persevering under trial.

Sometime later, the Jews seized Stephen and brought him to the Sanhedrin. This occurred shortly after the saints of God chose and ordained seven men to be the deacons in the church; Stephen was one of those men. At that time, a deacon's job was to make sure that the food was being evenly distributed throughout the body of Christ. He was brought before the Sanhedrin because the Jews lied on him by saying, "We have heard Stephen speak words of blasphemy against Moses and against God" (Acts 6:11, NIV). While he was standing before the Sanhedrin, the Jews spoke more lies about Stephen. But rather than defend himself against his accusers, Stephen preached a magnificent sermon to the Sanhedrin by perfectly quoting scriptures from the Tanakh (Old Testament).

Stephen talked about Abraham and stated that he became the father of Isaac; Isaac became the father of Jacob (Israel), and Jacob became the father of the twelve patriarchs. Then Stephen explained to the priests how the descendants of Israel would remain in Egypt until YHWH (usually rendered the Lord) would call and send Moses to be the ruler and deliverer of the Israelites. Stephen said, "He led them out of Egypt and did wonders and miraculous signs in Egypt, at the Red Sea and for forty years in the desert" (Acts 7:36, NIV). Stephen quoted Moses by saying, "God will send you a Prophet like me from your own people" (Acts 7:37, NIV). Jesus Christ is that prophet.

After he quoted Moses, Stephen told them that the Jews did not obey Moses and, in their hearts, turned back to Egypt (which represents the world and all of its lusts). Also, Stephen explained to the Sanhedrin how Moses, under the direction of God, commanded the Israelites to build the tabernacle of the testimony. He even quoted the prophet Isaiah by saying,

> Heaven is My throne, and the earth is My footstool. What kind of house will you build for Me? Says the Lord. Or where will My resting place be? Has not My hand made all these things? (Acts 7:49–50, NIV)

After Stephen preached his sermon, he called the members of the Sanhedrin stiff-necked people with uncircumcised hearts and ears. He told them that they are just like their disobedient ancestors who killed the first testament prophets, who predicted the first coming of the Messiah. And when Jesus finally revealed Himself to His own people, they disobeyed the Torah of Moses by rejecting and killing Him.

When the Sanhedrin heard what Stephen said to them, they became enraged. While this was happening, Stephen said, "Look! I see Heaven opened and the Son of Man standing at the right hand of God!" (Acts

7:56, Complete Jewish Bible) Stephen saw God's *Sh'khinah* (manifest glory, according to the Complete Jewish Bible), which was the Lord Jesus Christ standing at the highest position in heaven. They became so angry that they rushed at Stephen, dragged him out of the city, and began to stone him. The witnesses laid their clothes at the feet of a man named Saul; he was there, giving his approval to Stephen's murder. While they were stoning him, Stephen said, "Lord Jesus, receive my spirit" (Acts 7:59, NIV). Then he fell on his knees and cried out, "Lord, do not hold this sin against them" (Acts 7:60, NIV). Then he died. I hope you noticed how Stephen acted toward his enemies. He could've fought back with his fists or called down a curse on them in the name of the Lord. Instead of retaliating, he chose to pray for them. Stephen's prayer caused the Lord Jesus to spare the lives of the men who killed him, including the life of Saul. And very soon, you will read about the end result of Stephen's prayer for Saul. Stephen was the first saint of God to be killed because of his faith in the Lord Jesus.

On that same day, they buried the body of Stephen, and a great persecution broke out against the messianic community at Jerusalem. All the churches, except the apostles, were scattered throughout ancient Judea and Samaria. And to make things worse, Saul, one of the men Stephen prayed for, began to destroy the *ekklesia* (the church). Saul also put many of the saints in prison. But on the flipside, those who were scattered abroad preached the gospel of Christ wherever they went. Some days later, Philip, one of the original deacons, went to a city in Samaria and preached the word of God to the people. The Samaritans were a people of mixed blood. In other words, they were half Jewish and half gentile. A scholar by the name of G. W. Bromiley wrote the following:

> Philip's mission to Samaria brought many people to faith in Christ and these "were baptized, both men and women" (8:12). As Philip had preached "the good news about the

kingdom of God and the name of Jesus Christ," this baptism was given "in the name of the Lord Jesus."

Those Samaritans who heard and believed the gospel of God were baptized in the name of the Lord Jesus. When the apostles heard that the Samaritans had accepted the word of God, they sent Peter and John to them. When they arrived at that city, Peter and John prayed for those baptized Samaritans so that they would be filled with the Spirit of Christ. They laid their hands on each of them, and those Samaritans received the gift of the Holy Ghost. Their salvation was complete. Peter and John continued to preach the word of God in many Samarian villages.

Sometime later, an angel from heaven appeared to Philip and told him to go to Gaza. Along the way, he saw an Ethiopian eunuch sitting in his chariot and reading a passage of Scripture from the prophet Isaiah. The Lord told Philip to go to the chariot. He obeyed God and asked the eunuch, "Do you understand what you are reading?' (Acts 8:30, NASB).

The eunuch responded by saying, "How can I, unless someone explains it to me?" (Acts 8:31, NIV) . So the eunuch invited Philip on the chariot, and he sat with the eunuch. The eunuch was reading this passage of Scripture:

> He was led as a sheep to the slaughter; and like a lamb dumb before His shearer, so opened He not His mouth: in His humiliation His judgment was taken away: and who shall declare His generation? For His life is taken from the earth. (Acts 8:32–33, KJV)

The eunuch asked Philip, "Tell me, please, who is the prophet talking about, himself or someone else?" (Acts 8:34, NIV) . Then Philip began with that very passage of Scripture and preached the good news of Jesus. Now let me make a short point.

A lot of today's Christians fail to realize that the first-century church did not have the New Testament Scriptures when the church got started. These Jewish believers preached the gospel of Jesus the Messiah by quoting Scriptures from the Old Testament. The Jews and the church used the Hebrew Old Testament or the Greek Old Testament called the Septuagint. In fact, many of the churches didn't have the Tanakh. The saints that didn't have the Tanakh spread the gospel of Christ by word of mouth. Howbeit, the same Old Testament Scriptures that taught the Torah of Moses also taught that Jesus is the Christ. The Scriptures are truly inexhaustible.

Philip explained to the eunuch that Jesus is the Messiah and the Son of God. Also, Philip told the eunuch that he must be buried with Him through baptism. So when they came to a place where there was much water, the eunuch asked him, "Is there any reason why I shouldn't be immersed?" Then the eunuch stopped the chariot, and both of them went into the water. Philip baptized him in the name of the Lord Jesus. While both of them were still in the water, the Spirit of God took Philip away from the water, and God filled the eunuch with the Holy Ghost. When the eunuch came out of the water, not only was his salvation complete, he himself no longer saw Philip. Despite Philip's disappearance, the eunuch was not afraid; he got out of the water and went on his way rejoicing. Philip, however, appeared at Azotus (Ashdod), and he continued to preach the good news of Christ. William Baird, a professor of the New Testament at Texas Christian University located in Fort Worth, Texas, wrote the following:

> After the baptism, the Spirit sends Philip on his mission. Here some manuscripts say that the Spirit came on the eunuch and the angel caught up Philip. This would indicate that the Ethiopian has received the Holy Spirit at baptism.

Also, Christian Historian Marvin M. Arnold wrote the following in his outline:

> Acts 2:38 doctrine was taken to Ethiopia. Ethiopian Apostolic Christianity founded. It was later called North African Christianity; it spread through the continent. It never perished.

In other words, the gospel of Jesus and the apostle's doctrine are still being preached in Africa during the twenty-first century. This Ethiopian eunuch was the first gentile to be saved by the Lord Jesus.

Meanwhile, Saul was still destroying God's *ekklesia*. He went to the high priest in order to obtain permission to go to Damascus and search for any there who belonged to the Way. This is what the church was called at that time. If he found any of the saints there, he was going to put them in prison. The high priest granted him permission to go to Damascus. As Saul neared his destination, a brilliant light from heaven flashed around him and knocked him to the ground.

God called to him by saying, "Saul, Saul, why do you persecute Me?" (Acts 9:4, NIV).

"Who are you, *Kurios*? [Greek for *Lord*]" Saul asked. Then God said, "I am *Iēsoûs* [Greek for Jesus], whom you are persecuting" (Acts 9:5, NIV). Furthermore, Jesus said, "Now get up and go into the city, and you will be told what you must do" (Acts 9:6). The men traveling with Saul heard the voice from heaven, but they didn't see anyone. They had to help Saul get to Damascus because he was blinded by the light. In fact, Saul was blind for three days, and he didn't eat or drink anything.

At the same time, the Lord Jesus called to Ananias in a vision and said, "Go to the house of Judas on Straight Street and ask for a man from Tarsus named Saul, for he is praying. In a vision he has seen a man named Ananias come and place his hands on him to restore his sight" (Acts 9:11–12). Ananias was fearful of going anywhere near Saul because he heard of his reputation. But he obeyed the Lord and went to see Saul. He placed his hands on Saul, and then something like scales fell off Saul's eyes. Saul regained his sight, and Ananias baptized him in the name of Jesus the Messiah. Then God filled him with the Holy

Ghost. Not only did Saul receive salvation from the Lord, Stephen's prayer was answered by God. The Lord Jesus will go on to use Saul to preach to the gentiles, their kings, and to the Israelites. And Saul, who was a Pharisee, will suffer many hardships for the glory of God.

After spending several days with the disciples of Jesus in Damascus, Saul began to preach to the Jews that Jesus Christ is the Son of God. The Jews who heard him were astonished because the same man who wrecked havoc on God's *ekklesia* in Jerusalem was preaching and showing proof to the Jews that Yeshua is the Messiah. Because of Saul's preaching, the Jews in Damascus devised a plan to kill him. But Saul learned of their plan. He was able to escape the Jews because his followers lowered him in a basket through an opening in the wall. Saul immediately left Damascus and went into Arabia. It was there, in the desert, where the Lord Jesus revealed Himself to and instructed Saul on the doctrines of God. Then Saul left Arabia and returned to Damascus.

Three years later, Saul went to Jerusalem. He tried to join the disciples, but they were afraid of him. They didn't believe that he was a changed man. But Barnabas took hold of Saul and brought him to the apostles Peter and James, the Lord's younger brother according to the flesh. He described to them how Saul had seen the Lord on the road and that He had talked to him. Barnabas also described how Saul had spoken out boldly in the name of Jesus at Damascus. Peter and James accepted him as their brother in Christ. As a result, Saul stayed with them and moved about freely in Jerusalem, speaking boldly in the name of Jesus. He talked and debated with the Grecian Jews; as a result, they tried to kill him. When the brothers learned of this, they took Saul to Caesarea and sent him off to Tarsus. After Saul left Jerusalem, the church in ancient Judea enjoyed a time peace. The number of disciples, both men and women, increased day by day. And very soon, the Lord will add more gentiles into His messianic community.

THE SPREAD OF THE CHURCH

During the years AD 37–42, a missionary took the apostle's doctrine to ancient Glastonbury, England. This marks the beginning of Celtic Apostolic Christianity in England. Also, God sent Peter to Cornelius and his household to preach the good news of Jesus Christ. Cornelius was a gentile and a devout believer in the God of Israel, but he only knew God through the law of Moses. So Peter proclaimed to him that Jesus Christ is Lord of all, and he preached His death, burial, and resurrection. While Peter was still preaching, Cornelius and all the members of his house who heard Peter's message believed him so much that the Holy Ghost came on all of them. The Jewish believers who were with Peter were astonished because God had filled the gentiles in that place with the Holy Ghost as well. In fact, they know that those gentiles were filled with the Holy Ghost because they heard them speaking in tongues. Then Peter commanded them to be baptized in the name of Jesus the Messiah. So they went to a place where there was much water, and Peter baptized them in the name of Jesus Christ.

Peter and the Jewish believers were beginning to realize that God wants to save the gentiles as well as the Jews. But the messianic community as a whole didn't believe that the gentiles were worthy of this new life. So due to their prejudice against the gentiles, God continued to deal with His church on this issue. For example, the churches that were scattered by the persecution against them at Jerusalem traveled as far as ancient Phoenicia, Cyprus, and Antioch. They were preaching the gospel of Christ only to Jews. But God got a hold of some Jewish saints from Cyprus and Cyrene and sent them to Antioch. These men told the message of salvation to the Jews and gentiles. As a result, a great number of people believed the gospel of Christ, and the Lord filled them with the Holy Ghost.

Barnabas met with Saul, and they went to the church in Antioch. They spent a whole year with the church in Antioch, and they taught a multitude of people. During this period of time, the saints of God, for the first time, were called Christians at Antioch. Throughout history, we will be called many names by the enemies of God. But I'll bring this out later on in this book.

During the year AD 44, King Herod persecuted the church by arresting some of the saints of God. He even arrested the apostle James, who was the brother of the apostle John. King Herod killed James by cutting off his head. The emissary James was the first of the original eleven to be martyred during the first century. Then there were only eleven out of the twelve chosen apostles who were still alive. To make things worse, the apostle Peter was arrested and put in prison. While he was in prison, the church was earnestly praying to God for him. And because of their prayers, an angel from heaven came down to the place where Peter was located and literally busted Peter out of prison. Then Peter went to the house of Mark's mother in order to tell the saints that he was out of prison. When they opened the door and saw Peter, they became ecstatic. Peter calmed them down and described to them how the Lord Jesus had brought him out of prison. Also, Peter said, "Tell James [the Lord's younger half-brother] and the brothers about this" (Acts 12:17). Then he left for another place. The next morning, King Herod searched for Peter and didn't find him. As a result, Herod cross-examined the guards and ordered that they be executed. Sometime later, the Lord sent an angel to smite and kill King Herod. You don't mess with the saints of God and get away with it.

The word of God continued to spread throughout ancient Palestine. Many souls were baptized in the name of Jesus Christ and filled with the Holy Ghost. In addition, Peter fled to Babylon located in ancient Mesopotamia around AD 45. He taught the doctrine of Christ in that area, and it spread to the Far East region of Asia. Peter's apostleship and ministry was with the Jews, not the gentiles. In fact, history shows that there were as many Jews living in the Mesopotamian areas in Christ's time as there were in ancient Judea. So throughout his ministry, Peter traveled through the Asian areas of Judea, Syria, Mesopotamia, and possibly Arabia. Now let's get back to the story.

Saul and Barnabas were still in Antioch, Syria. When they had finished their ministry in Antioch, they went to Jerusalem. After a very short visit to Jerusalem, Saul and Barnabas returned to the church in Antioch.

During the year AD 47, Saul, a.k.a. Paul, began his first missionary journey throughout the Roman Empire. He and Barnabas, sent on their way by the Holy Ghost, went to a city in ancient Syria and sailed from there to Cyprus. Cyprus is an island located in the Mediterranean Sea west of Syria. Also, John (a.k.a. Mark) was with them. When they arrived at Salamis, a city located in Cyprus, they preached the word of God to the people. They traveled through the whole island until they came to the city of Paphos. As a result of their preaching, Cyprus was Christianized with the apostle's doctrine. Then Paul and his companions sailed from Paphos to Perga located in ancient Pamphylia. While they were in Perga, Mark left them to return to Jerusalem. After this happened, Paul and Barnabas went to Antioch of Pisidia and preached the word of God to the Jews and God-fearing gentiles. Many of the gentiles became believers and the word of God spread throughout that whole region. The Holy Ghost was being poured out on those gentiles!

Paul and Barnabas traveled through the cities of Iconium and Lystra. They proclaimed the word of the Lord in those cities. The Lord Jesus performed many miracles and saved many souls through Paul and Barnabas. And while Paul was in Lystra, he suffered for the name of Jesus. This happened because some of the Jews from Antioch and Iconium, who rejected the gospel of Christ, came to that city and won the crowd over. They caused the people to stone Paul and drag him outside the city. They left him there to die. But after the disciples had gathered around him and prayed, he got up and went back into the city. Paul was a bold man for Christ. The next day, Paul and Barnabas went to the city of Derbe and proclaimed the good news of God. They won a multitude of souls, and the number of disciples in that city increased greatly. They also preached to the people located in the surrounding country in that area. Then they returned to each of the cities where they had proclaimed the gospel so that they could strengthen and encourage the disciples. They said to them, "Through many tribulations we must enter the kingdom of God" (Acts 14:22, NASB).

This is a true statement for all the saints of God. We should not be surprised when we experience many kinds of trials and troubles in this life. The Lord Yeshua allows these things to happen to us in order to strengthen and transform us into better saints. Also, He does this in order to prepare us for the world to come. Paul and Barnabas ordained elders for them in each church in those cities, and they went back to Perga and preached the gospel. Then they sailed back to Antioch located in Syria. When they arrived, they gathered the messianic community together and told them how God had opened the door of faith to the gentiles. Paul's first missionary journey was finished.

During the year AD 49, the *ekklesia* had its first council in Jerusalem. This happened because some men from Judea went to the church at Antioch, Syria and began to teach the saints: "Unless you are circumcised, according to the custom taught by Moses, you cannot be saved." They were teaching this to the Gentile believers. So in order to address the question about circumcision, Paul and Barnabas went to the council in Jerusalem and met with the elders and the other apostles.

After much discussion, Peter got up and addressed them. He said, "Now then, why do you try to test God by putting on the necks of the disciples a yoke that neither we nor our fathers have been able to bear? No! We believe it is through the grace of our Lord Jesus that we are saved, just as they are" (Acts 15:10–11, NIV). After he said these words, Paul and Barnabas explained to them how God had worked with them among the gentiles.

Then James (the Lord's brother) spoke to the members of the council. He said, "We should write to them, telling them to abstain from food polluted by idols, from sexual immorality, from the meat of strangled animals and from blood" (Acts 15:20, NIV). So the council wrote a letter to the gentile believers in Antioch, Syria, and Cilicia, and they chose Barsabbas and Silas to go with Paul and Barnabas to Antioch. When they arrived at Antioch, they gathered the messianic community there and delivered the letter to them. After spending some time in Antioch, Barsabbas went back to Jerusalem. Sometime later, Paul wanted to go back to the cities where he had established churches and see how they were doing. Barnabas wanted to take Mark with them, but Paul didn't want Mark to join them because Mark deserted them during their first missionary journey. So Barnabas took Mark with him and sailed to Cyprus, and Paul took Silas with him and went through the churches in Syria and Cilicia.

It is believed by most Christian scholars that James, the Lord's brother according to the flesh, wrote his epistle around AD 45–50. This God-breathed letter was addressed to the churches that were dispersed throughout the known world at that time. In his letter, James wrote, "What use is it, my brethren, if a man says he has faith, but he has no works? Can that faith save him?" (James 2:14, NASB). The lesson to be learned is this: faith without deeds being performed as a result of your faith is not faith in God at all! This is why James wrote, "For just as the body without the spirit is dead, so also faith without works is dead" (James 2:26, NASB). Also, James said, "Anyone, then, who knows the good he ought to do and doesn't do it, sins." Saints of God, we must examine ourselves and do the right thing. And prior to writing his closing remarks, James wrote that we must patiently wait for the coming of the Lord.

Paul wrote his letter to the churches in Galatia around AD 48–56. God inspired him to write this letter because some Judaizers were causing the gentile believers to depart from the faith. In his letter, Paul wrote,

> I am amazed that you are so quickly deserting Him who called you by the grace of Christ, for a different gospel; which is really not another; only there are some who are disturbing you, and want to distort the gospel of Christ. But even though we, or an angel from Heaven, should preach to you a gospel contrary to that which we have preached to you, let him be accursed. (Gal. 1:6–8, NASB)

Anyone who continues to preach a different gospel of Christ or a religious doctrine that has nothing to do with the deity of Christ will be eternally damned! And throughout the rest of this letter, Paul explained to the Galatians the freedom that they have in the Messiah. The grace of Christ has set us free from the ceremonial laws of the Old Testament. This letter helped the churches in Galatia to return to the grace of God, and their faith in Jesus was strengthened.

Paul began his second missionary journey throughout the Roman Empire in AD 49. He returned to Lystra and met Timothy, the one who will later receive two divine letters from Paul. Timothy joined Paul, Luke (a gentile proselyte who got saved), and Silas as they traveled from Lystra to ancient Macedonia. When they came to the city of Philippi, they witnessed to a group of women. Lydia, who was one of the women who heard Paul's gospel, responded to his message of salvation. She and her whole household were baptized, and God filled them with the Holy Ghost. Sometime later, Paul and Silas were met by a servant girl who was possessed by a demonic spirit. The spirit that was in her helped her to predict the future, and she made money for her owners by fortune-telling. Perhaps this explains why some people can tell a person's future. She followed Paul and Silas and kept on saying, "These men are bond-servants of the Most High God, who are proclaiming to you the way of salvation" (Acts 16:17, NASB). She kept this up for many days. Paul became so irritated by that unclean spirit that he commanded that spirit to come out of her in the name of Jesus the Messiah. Once the owners of the servant girl realized that they cannot make anymore money off her, they seized Paul and Silas, brought them to the authorities, and flogged them. They were also put in prison.

Paul and Silas had every reason to complain to God about their current predicament because they suffered punishment at the hands of evil men for doing the right thing. After all, saints are supposed to cast out demonic spirits. But instead of complaining, at midnight, Paul and Silas began to pray to the Lord Jesus and praise Him by singing spiritual songs. As a result of their praise, God caused an earthquake to happen. Immediately the chains that were holding all the prisoners were loosed, and the prison doors were opened. When the jailer, the one responsible for keeping the prisoners, woke up and saw that the prison doors were opened, he thought that the prisoners had escaped. If his boss would've found out about this, the jailer would suffer severe consequences. He was so afraid that he tried to kill himself with his sword. But Paul shouted, "Don't harm yourself! We are all here!" (Acts 16:28, NIV).

The jailer ran to Paul and Silas and said, "Sirs, what must I do to be saved?"

They replied, "Believe in the Lord Jesus, and you shall be saved, you and your household" (Acts 16:30–31, NASB). Then they spoke to the jailer the details about how to get saved. And at that same hour of the night, the jailer and his family were immersed, in water, in the name of the Lord Jesus. Then God filled them with the Holy Ghost. This is the beginning of the church in Philippi. Even though they suffered, God used Paul and Silas to establish His ekklesia in Philippi.

After Paul and Silas were released from prison, they traveled to the city of Thessalonica. They preached the gospel of Christ in that city, and many Jews and gentiles were saved by the Lord Jesus. They received the Holy Ghost just like the rest of the saints. But the Jews were so angry at their preaching that they caused a riot in Thessalonica. The

Jews accused Paul and Silas of turning the world upside down with their message. But in reality they were turning the world right side up again; for God did create humankind to worship Him. The Jews tried to seize Paul and Silas, but they were able to hide from the Jews. They traveled to Berea and preached the gospel in that city. Paul and his brothers in Christ established churches in both cities. Then Paul traveled to the city of ancient Athens. While he was there, Paul preached a magnificent sermon at a meeting of the Areopagus. His sermon is my favorite passage of Scripture. He covered many subjects, including the resurrection of Jesus Christ. Several people of Athens heard his sermon and became followers of Paul. They believed in the Lord Jesus and were baptized.

After they won more souls in Athens, Paul, Silas, Luke, and Timothy went to Corinth to preach the good news of God. Many of the Corinthians who heard them believed in the Lord and were baptized. After staying in Corinth for over eighteen months, Paul left his brothers and sailed to Caesarea. While on his way there, Paul arrived at Ephesus and tried to reason with some Jews concerning Jesus in a synagogue. They wanted him to spend some more time with them, but Paul declined. He told them that he will return to Ephesus if it's God's will. Then Paul sailed from Ephesus to Caesarea. He greeted the messianic community there, and then he traveled back to Antioch, Syria. Paul finished his second missionary journey in AD 52.

During AD 51–52, while Paul was still in Corinth, he wrote two letters to the churches in Thessalonica. Silas and Timothy aided Paul in writing these God-breathed letters. The apostle Paul had received a revelation from God regarding the destiny of His church. In his letter, Paul said,

> For this we say to you by the word of the Lord, that we who are alive, and remain until the coming of the Lord, shall not precede those who have fallen asleep. For the Lord Himself will descend from Heaven with a shout, with the voice of

the archangel, and with the trumpet of God; and the dead in Christ shall rise first. Then we who are alive and remain shall be caught up together with them in the clouds to meet the Lord in the air, and thus we shall always be with the Lord. Therefore comfort one another with these words. (1 Thess. 4:15–18, NASB)

This is so awesome! The Lord showed me in a dream what the apostle was talking about. I tell the truth and lie not.

During the summer of 2008, I had a dream that I was in an empty space in the universe that was far above all the galaxies. I could see the galaxies below me, and there was nothing but dark matter in front of and above me. All of a sudden, a door of pure white light opened from left to right, and I saw a Man fly through the opening downward toward the universe. It was Jesus Christ descending through the universe, and millions of brown balls of light followed Him. These are the dead in Christ.

The Lord had dark-brown hair. In fact, He had a short Jewfro. He had brown-colored skin similar to a Latin-American man or a man from the Middle East. In other words, He looked like a brown-skinned Palestinian Jew. He had a beard and mustache altogether. Also, He was wearing the type of clothes that a priest or a king would wear. The colors of His clothes were white, blue, and purple. This is the best way that I can describe what I saw in my dream.

In one scene, Jesus was descending toward the right. In another scene, I saw Him descending toward the left. And I saw blue galaxies, red galaxies, yellow galaxies, white galaxies, purple galaxies, and more galaxies with different colors. The Lord kept descending until He reached earth. I saw our planet frozen in time. When He reached our atmosphere, the dead in Christ stayed in space just above our atmosphere. While the Lord was descending toward earth, I saw the nations of modern-day Egypt, Israel, Jordan, and Lebanon. He descended into Israel, and then He stopped right above Mount Olivet. And I heard the

Lord in plain English when He shouted, "Come up here!" After He said these words, all the dead in Christ changed into images and balls of white light! And the saints of God who were still alive on earth ascended into the sky. As we got closer to the Lord, we were changing into images and balls of white light! The saints ascended to where He was in Israel, and we were gathered to meet Him in the clouds! Then the Lord Jesus shot up like a surface-to-air missile. He soared high into the universe, and I saw all these white balls of light following Him. These white balls of light are the original and primitive ekklesia.

In one scene, He was ascending toward the right. In another scene, I saw Him ascending toward the left. And in another scene, I saw Jesus vertically ascending with all of these white balls of light following Him. I was among those who were caught up, but at the same time, I was seeing all of this happening at a distance. And I saw green galaxies, red galaxies, orange galaxies, and many other galaxies that God had created in His universe! Then Jesus entered into that same empty space in the universe, which is far above the galaxies. That door of pure white light was open, and the Lord was soaring toward that door. The Lord was getting closer and closer to that door. And when He was about to enter into heaven, I woke up from that dream. Glory to King Jesus! Thank you, Lord Jesus Christ! The Lord our God is awesome! Hold on, saints of God. We are almost there! When Paul finished writing his letter, he sent it to the Thessalonian church.

A few months later, some bad characters rose up within the Thessalonian church and told the saints that they have already missed the day of the Lord (the rapture) . The word of this happening to the Thessalonians reached the apostle Paul. In order to prevent a complete overthrowing of their faith, God inspired Paul to write a second letter to the Thessalonian church. In his letter, Paul stated that the day of the Lord has not come yet, for God is holding back the man of sin (the Antichrist). Paul wrote the following: "And you know what restrains him now, so that in his time he may be revealed. For the mystery of lawlessness is already at work; only He who now restrains will do so until He is taken out of the way. And then that lawless one will be revealed" (2 Thess. 2:6–8, NASB). The Antichrist won't be revealed until the Holy Ghost, through His ministry and presence in His saints, is taken out of this world. And when this happens, the whole world will be in trouble. After Paul finished writing his second letter to the Thessalonians, he sent it to them. This letter restored and strengthened the faith of the saints at Thessalonica. And the Lord will continue to use Paul in a mighty way throughout his ministry.

In addition, during the AD 50s, the apostle Thaddaeus (a.k.a. Judas) traveled to ancient Armenia and established the church in that area. Also, the apostle Thomas traveled to Malabar, India, and established the ekklesia in that area. The church continued to spread throughout Europe, Asia, and Africa. And more revelations from God are still to come.

After spending some time in Antioch, Syria, Paul set out from there and began his third missionary journey. He traveled throughout the region of Galatia and Phrygia, strengthening all the disciples. Meanwhile, a Jew named Apollos came to Ephesus and taught from the Old Testament Scriptures that Jesus is the Messiah. But there was a problem: he only knew the baptism of John the Immerser. Two saints named Priscilla and Aquila heard him speak in a synagogue. After they heard him speak to the Jews, they invited him to their home and explained to him the way of God more adequately. Then Apollos was baptized in the name of the Lord Jesus Christ, and God filled him with the Holy Ghost. When Apollos was completely converted, he went to the region of Achaia and used the Tanakh to prove to the Jews that Jesus is the Messiah.

Sometime later, Paul traveled back to Ephesus and found some disciples of John the Baptizer. Paul asked them, "Have you received the Holy Ghost since you believed?" And they said to him, "We have not so much as heard whether there be any Holy Ghost." So Paul asked them how were they baptized, and they told him John's baptism. Then Paul said, "John verily baptized with the baptism of repentance, saying unto the people, that they should believe on Him which should come after him, that is, on Christ [the Messiah] Jesus" (Acts 19:2–4, KJV). When they heard this, they humbled themselves, and Paul baptized them in the name of the Lord Jesus. Then the Holy Ghost came on them, and they began to speak in tongues and prophesy. The *Encyclopedia Britannica* further explains what just occurred by stating the following:

> We gather from Acts xix. 4, that John had merely baptized in the name of the coming Messiah, without identifying him with Jesus of Nazareth.

Also, the *Encyclopedia Britannica* says,

> On the other hand, in Acts xix. 1–7, twelve disciples, for such they were already accounted, who had been baptized into John's baptism, *i.e.* into the name of him that should follow John, but had not even heard of the Holy Spirit, are at Paul's instance re-baptized into the name of the Lord Jesus.

Furthermore, Thomas Weisser, an anointed man of God and the author of *Jesus' Name Baptism through the Centuries*, wrote the following:

> Considering the significance of being baptized "into the name," Ralph Bohlmann has shed some light on early practices. After outlining the meaning of entering into union with God through baptism he explains another aspect. "Another explanation is suggested on the basis of many of the papyri coming from the Hellenistic world of business and finance. Here the expression "into the name" was used to designate an entry made into an account or account book over which the name of the owner was written. What was placed "into the name" of a person was placed into his account and became his possession.

The apostles and disciples of Christ baptized new converts into the name of Jesus so that God would put His purchased possession into His account book: the book of life. Also, the apostles invoked the name of Jesus whenever they baptized a sinner because the Name is in the blood and the blood is in the Name! To be baptized in the name of Jesus was imperative during the first century, and it is still imperative in the twenty-first century. So it doesn't matter how you try to interpret the Scriptures, for you cannot deny the fact that the New Testament teaches water baptism in the name of Jesus. Paul would stay in Ephesus for the next two years preaching the gospel of God to the Jews and gentiles.

Around AD 55, Paul wrote his first letter to the Corinthian church. God inspired him to write this letter because Paul received the word about what was happening at that church. The saints were acting like fools in Corinth. There was division in the church, a man had slept with his father's wife (his stepmother), and the saints were speaking in tongues just for the sake of speaking in tongues during church services. So Paul wrote a detailed letter to them, which covered various topics, from divisions in the church to the rapture of the church. In his letter, Paul said,

> Do you not know that the unrighteous shall not inherit the kingdom of God? Do not be deceived; neither fornicators, nor idolaters, nor adulterers, nor effeminate, nor homosexuals, nor thieves, nor the covetous, nor drunkards, nor revilers, nor swindlers, shall inherit the kingdom of God. And such were some of you; but you were washed, but you were sanctified, but you were justified in the name of the Lord Jesus Christ, and in the Spirit of our God. (1 Cor. 6:9–11, NASB). Glory to King Jesus! I know God loves me! And God loves everyone, including His precious saints.

Paul went on to write about marriage, communion, the spiritual gifts that God gives to His saints, and the true meaning of *agape* (Greek for the love that comes from God). Paul also wrote, "He that speaks in an unknown tongue speaks not unto men, but unto God: for no man understands him; howbeit in the Spirit he speaks mysteries. But he that prophesies speaks unto men to edification, and exhortation, and comfort. He that speaks in an unknown tongue edifies himself; but he that prophesies edifies the church" (1 Cor. 14:2–4, KJV). *Oikodomeo* is the Greek word for edification, and this is where the word *edify* comes from. Edify means "the act of building; the promotion of spiritual growth" (W.E. Vine). Speaking in tongues is a powerful force for promoting spiritual growth. It gives saints refreshing and rest in trying situations, and it builds up and strengthens our faith in God. Also, speaking in tongues is one of the most powerful proofs of God's existence and the truthfulness of the Bible. This is why Satan, through vain men, is always trying to deceive us into thinking that speaking in tongues isn't real. After all, the devil does not want us to have power over him and his army of demonic spirits. I've made my point, so let's get back to the story. When Paul finished his letter, he sent it to the Corinthian church.

The Lord Jesus used Paul to win many souls, and He performed extraordinary miracles through him. In fact, the church in Ephesus increased so much that the worship of the goddess Artemis (in the Latin tongue Diana) was dwindling. So some bad characters caused a riot in that city. They did this because of the church and its influence on the citizens of that city. When the riot had ended, Paul left Ephesus and traveled through Macedonia and ancient Greece. While Paul was in these nations, he encouraged the saints and preached the gospel of Christ. Then Paul went to a city called Miletus, and he sent to Ephesus for the elders of the church. When the elders from Ephesus arrived at Miletus, Paul spoke many encouraging words to them and bade them farewell. Paul said, "Take heed therefore unto yourselves, and to all the flock, over the which the Holy Ghost has made you overseers, to feed the church of God, which He has purchased with His own blood" (Acts

20:28, kjv). After Paul encouraged the elders, he and his companions traveled all the way back to the city of Tyre. Paul stayed in Tyre for a short period of time, and then he traveled to Jerusalem. So around AD 56, Paul finished his third missionary journey.

Around AD 56, while Paul was still in Macedonia, he wrote his second letter to the Corinthian church. God inspired Paul to write this letter to the Corinthians in order to give them further instructions in righteousness and to address the problems that still persisted in that church. In his letter, Paul wrote the following: "Therefore if any man be in Christ, he is a new creature: old things are passed away; behold, all things are become new. And all things are of God, who has reconciled us to Himself by Jesus Christ, and has given to us the ministry of reconciliation" (2 Cor. 5:17–18, kjv). All of God's saints are ambassadors for Christ, not the pope! And it is up to us to complete our ministry in Christ by winning souls.

Paul goes on to exhort the saints at Corinth to be holy and to show generosity towards others in need. Then Paul tells the saints that he has been whipped thirty -nine times on five different occasions and beaten with rods on three different occasions because of his preaching. I believe that the reason why Paul was so dedicated to serve the Lord, despite all of his hardships, is because of the glimpse of heaven that God had showed him. Paul wrote about it in his letter. Once Paul saw what heaven looks like, he became determined to finish his race. After all, the Lord Jesus told Paul what was awaiting him in each city where he would preach the gospel; God showed him that his hardships and sufferings are nothing when compared to the glory that awaits him in Paradise. Not just him, but every saint who endures unto the end. When Paul finished writing his letter, he sent it to the Corinthians through a saint named Titus.

During that same year, Paul wrote the most profound book that is in the New Testament canon: his epistle to the Romans. There are so many good spiritual lessons in this epistle. Paul begins his letter by writing the following:

> Paul, a servant of Jesus Christ, called to be an apostle, separated unto the gospel of God, (which He had promised afore by His prophets in the holy Scriptures,) concerning His Son Jesus Christ our Lord, which was made of the seed of David according to the flesh; and declared to be the Son of God with power, according to the Spirit of holiness, by the resurrection from the dead. (Rom. 1:1–4, KJV)

Look at how Paul breaks down and explains the dual nature of Jesus Christ. Paul goes on to write the following:

> The wrath of God is being revealed from heaven against all the godlessness and wickedness of men who suppress the truth by their wickedness, since what may be known about God is plain to them, because God has made it plain to them. For since the creation of the world God's invisible qualities—His eternal power and Divine nature—have been clearly seen, being understood from what has been made, so that men are without excuse. (Rom. 1:18–20, NIV)

It is too obvious that God exists. And if you don't believe in God, then God Himself calls you a fool.

In the same letter, Paul wrote,

> What if some did not have faith? Will their lack of faith nullify God's faithfulness? Not at all! Let God be true, and every man a liar. As it is written: "So that You may be proved right when You speak and prevail when You judge." But if our unrighteousness brings out God's righteousness more clearly, what shall we say? That God is unjust in bringing His wrath on us? (I am using a human argument.) Certainly not! If that were so, how could God judge the world? Someone

might argue, "If my falsehood enhances God's truthfulness and so increases His glory, why am I still condemned as a sinner?" Why not say—as we are being slanderously reported as saying and as some claim that we say—"Let us do evil that good may result"? Their condemnation is deserved. (Rom. 3:3–8, NIV)

This is awesome stuff! He's saying that if you suppress the truth of God, God's truth becomes more obvious. So the sinner can't win. Paul also wrote, "However, you are not in the flesh but in the Spirit, if indeed the Spirit of God dwells in you. But if anyone does not have the Spirit of Christ, he does not belong to Him" (Rom. 8:9, NASB). If you have not received the gift of the Holy Ghost according to the Scriptures, then you will be sent to hell after you die. I'm only telling you this because I love you. Repent and receive the Holy Ghost! Paul also talks about baptism, life through the Spirit, and Israel's destiny. And last but not least, Paul tells the saints of God to be holy. When Paul finished writing his letter, he sent it to the saints living in ancient Rome.

While he was in Jerusalem, a series of unfortunate but prophetic events landed Paul in Caesarea. Paul stood trial before Felix, the governor of Judea. He was on trial because the Jews had accused Paul of being a troublemaker among them all over the known world. Also, they accused Paul of desecrating the temple. The Jews were still living as if they were under the law of Moses during this period of time. They were even performing animal sacrifices. After they stated their accusations against Paul to Felix, Paul spoke and defended himself against the Jews. Paul also spoke to Felix about the Messiah Jesus and the kingdom of God for two years. During the year AD 58, Felix was succeeded by Porcius Festus. Soon after this happened, Paul decided to appeal to Caesar, who was Emperor Nero (AD 54–68) at that time.

Paul would later give his testimony about how the Lord Jesus saved him before Governor Festus and King Agrippa. When King Agrippa had determined that Paul had not done anything that was worthy of death, he sent Paul to Rome, Italy, because of his appeal to Caesar. When Paul arrived at Rome, he was given a rented house to live in and a Roman soldier to guard him. This is Paul's first imprisonment in Rome. Paul preached the good news of Christ to the Jews and gentiles. Some of the Jews who heard Paul's message were persuaded by what he said to them. They were eventually baptized. But most of the Jews rejected Paul's message of salvation. Luke was with Paul throughout his journey to and his stay in Rome, and Paul stayed in that rented house for two years.

For almost thirty years after Christ's ascension into heaven, the messianic community did not have any of the four gospels of Jesus in writing. The story of the Messiah's life was mostly spread by word of mouth. But this changed during the years of AD 55–59; this is when the apostle Levi (a.k.a. Matthew) wrote his account of the life of Jesus Christ. God inspired Matthew to write this book so that the church would have a deeper understanding of who Jesus Christ is in writing.

For instance, Matthew wrote about Mary, who was a virgin and Jewess maiden. She is the one who fulfilled the prophecy of the prophet Isaiah concerning the virgin who would give birth to the everlasting Father incarnate. The Holy Ghost, who is also God the Father, is the One who caused the conception of the Son of God inside of Mary's womb. When she gave birth to the Holy Child, Joseph (Mary's fiancé) named Him Yeshua because God commanded him to give Him that name. The word *Yeshua* is a combination of the Hebrew word and verb for *save* and God's Old Testament name *YHWH*. So the name of Jesus means "YHWH saves, YHWH redeems, and YHWH delivers." The name of Jesus also means "Jehovah is become my salvation." The name of YHWH still endures to this very day through the name of Jesus. The Messiah Jesus is YHWH incarnate, and Jesus is the name of the God of Israel and His Son! Even as a baby, Yeshua was *Immanuel*, which is Hebrew for "God with us" (Matt. 1:23).

When Jesus Christ became a grown man, He began His earthly ministry. Also, Jesus chose His original twelve disciples. Later on in his book, Matthew wrote that Peter confessed that Jesus is the Messiah and the Son of God. After Peter made this confession, Jesus said the following to him:

> "And I say also unto you, that you are Peter, and upon this rock I will build My church, and the gates of Hell shall not prevail against it" (Matt. 16:18, kjv).

The fact that Jesus is the Messiah is the foundation of God's ekklesia. This passage of Scripture is the inspiration of my book; for God has sustained the apostle's doctrine throughout the centuries. Matthew concludes his book by writing his version of Christ's crucifixion, the resurrection of Jesus, and the Great Commission. Jesus said, "Go ye therefore, and teach all nations, baptizing them in the name of the Father, and of the Son, and of the Holy Ghost: teaching them to observe all things whatsoever I have commanded you: and, lo, I am with you always, even unto the end of the world. Amen" (Matt. 28:19, kjv). The same apostle who wrote this book has been baptizing new converts in the name of Jesus Christ since the day of Pentecost. And after he wrote his book, Matthew continued to baptize sinners in the name of Jesus Christ. This is the truth. So repent, humble yourself, and embrace the apostle's doctrine!

Around AD 60, Luke wrote his version of the gospel of Jesus the Messiah. God inspired Luke to write this book because the church needed more facts about the life of Jesus. In his book, Luke gives us a more detailed story of the virgin birth of Jesus, and he tells us some of the things that the Son of Man did when He was twelve years old. Also, Luke tells us where Jesus lived. For instance, Luke wrote the following: "When they had performed everything according to the Law of the Lord, they returned to Galilee, to their own city of Nazareth. And the

Child continued to grow and become strong, increasing in wisdom; and the grace of God was upon Him" (Luke 2:39–40, NASB).

Luke also wrote, "Then He went down to Nazareth with them and was obedient to them. But His mother treasured all these things in her heart. And Jesus grew in wisdom and stature, and in favor with God and men" (Luke 2:51–52, NIV). Jesus lived in a town called Nazareth until He was about thirty years old. During this period of time, Yeshua did not leave Nazareth to go to India, and He didn't live anywhere else! You'd be surprised to hear the many theories about what Jesus did during His so-called "silent years." According to Luke, Jesus said, "The one who listens to you listens to Me, and the one who rejects you rejects Me; and he who rejects Me rejects the One who sent Me" (Luke 10:16, NASB). The saints of God are the representatives for Christ. So anyone who rejects what Peter and the other apostles said, including our testimony about the Lord Jesus, rejects God.

Luke goes on to write about the crucifixion of the Anointed One. It is Luke who wrote about Jesus forgiving a criminal who was crucified along with Him. So many false Christians try to use this passage of Scripture in order to prove that baptism saves nobody. But they forget that Jesus Christ was crucified during the dispensation of the law. David K. Bernard, my brother in Christ Jesus, wrote the following:

> During the time of Jesus' earthly ministry, He upheld the old covenant as the path to eternal life (Luke 10:25–28) and commanded His followers to obey the Law of Moses (Matthew 19:16–19; 23:1–3, 23). He told an adulteress, "Go, and sin no more" (John 8:11), leaving her with the Law as a moral guide. He told one leper He healed, "Go thy way, show thyself to the priest, and offer the gift that Moses commanded" (Matthew 8:4), and He told ten other lepers, "Go shew yourselves unto the priests" (Luke 17:14). Those who accepted Christ's message were saved under the old covenant while they waited for the new covenant and the

promised Holy Spirit. They were saved in harmony with the Law, not in contradiction to it. For example, Jesus served as both sacrificial lamb and high priest for the thief on the cross. Before Pentecost, God expected people to follow the Law; after Pentecost God expects them to follow the gospel for the New Testament church age.

While Jesus Christ was on the cross, He was shedding His innocent blood as the Lamb of God and performing His role as the thief's High Priest and God according to the Torah. These are the reasons why the Messiah forgave the thief on the cross. But on the Day of Pentecost, God established the church age; all sinners must repent, be baptized in the name of Jesus Christ, and be filled with the Holy Ghost. Luke concludes his book by writing his version of the resurrection of Jesus, the Great Commission of Jesus, and Christ's ascension into heaven. And around AD 61, Luke wrote The Acts of the Holy Ghost, which is believed to be the original title of his second book. Today, Luke's second book is titled The Acts of the Apostles, or The Book of Acts. This book is the record of the first thirty years of the church age, and it tells us how to obtain salvation through our Lord Jesus Christ.

THE FIRST CENTURY, PART 2

Paul was imprisoned in Rome around AD 60–62. While Paul was in Rome, he wrote four different God-breathed letters to the churches. One of them was his letter to the saints located in ancient Colossae. In his letter, Paul wrote the following about the Son of God: He is the image of the invisible God, the firstborn over all creation. For by Him all things were created: things in heaven and on earth, visible and invisible, whether thrones or powers or rulers or authorities; all things were created by Him and for Him. He is before all things, and in Him all things hold together" (Col. 1:15–17, NASB).

Paul also wrote, "See to it that no one takes you captive through hollow and deceptive philosophy, which depends on human tradition and the basic principles of this world rather than on Christ. For in Christ all the fullness of the Deity lives in bodily form, and you have been given fullness in Christ, who is the Head over every power and authority" (Col. 2:8–10, NASB). Then Paul wrote, "And whatever you do, whether in word or deed, do it all in the name of the Lord Jesus, giving thanks to God the Father through Him" (Col. 3:17, NIV). The words of Paul speak for themselves. After Paul wrote this letter, he sent it to the Colossian church.

Paul's next letter was his epistle to the messianic community at Ephesus. Paul wrote this letter to encourage and strengthen the saints. In his letter, Paul wrote, "In whom you also trusted, after that you heard the word of truth, the gospel of your salvation: in whom also after that you believed, you were sealed with that Holy Spirit of promise, which is the earnest of our inheritance until the redemption of the purchased possession, unto the praise of His glory" (Eph. 1:13–14, KJV).

Receiving the gift of the Holy Ghost is our guarantee that we are saved right now in this life. All we have to do is be holy, for God is holy. Paul tells us that we are saved by the grace of God and that the saints are one in the Messiah Jesus. Also, Paul wrote that there is "one Lord, one faith, one baptism, one God and Father of all, who is above all, and through all, and in you all" (Eph. 4:4–5, KJV). The Holy Ghost is God the Father dwelling in His saints. Paul tells us the purposes of the fivefold ministry. He goes on to write about the fact that the Christian marriage is the earthly representation of the relationship between Christ and His church. Paul also gives specific commands to all Christian husbands and wives; if the saints who are married follow his commands, then their marriage will be blessed and honored by God. If you're married, you might as well be happily married. Prior to the apostle finishing his letter, he tells the saints to put on the armor of God so that we can stand against the trickery of the devil. After Paul finished his epistle, he sent it to the ekklesia at Ephesus.

Soon after Paul sent his letter to the saints at Ephesus, he wrote a letter to his dear friend Philemon. He did this because of Onesimus, who was a male slave who belonged to Philemon. Apparently, Onesimus had stolen some goods from his master and fled to Rome. When he reached Rome, Onesimus met Paul while he was in prison. Paul witnessed to him, and then Onesimus was baptized and filled with the Holy Ghost. After his conversion, Onesimus became a valuable helper of Paul in spreading the gospel. But Paul wanted to send him back to Philemon.

In his letter, Paul wrote, "For perhaps he was for this reason parted from you for a while, that you should have him back forever, no longer as a slave, but more than a slave, a beloved brother, especially to me, but how much more to you, both in the flesh and in the Lord" (Philemon 1:15–16, NASB). Love and forgiveness are the central themes in this epistle. After all, the Lord that we serve is a friend who sticks closer to us than a brother or sister. When Paul finished his letter, he sent it to Philemon. Onesimus was also sent back to his master and brother in the Lord.

Sometime later, Paul wrote a letter to the Philippian church. Paul did this around AD 61–62. In his letter, Paul commands the saints to imitate Christ's humility. Even though the Son of God is the Lord from heaven, Jesus humbled Himself and became obedient until the day He died. And when God raised the Messiah from the dead, He exalted the Son of God to the highest position in heaven. So if we live the way Jesus lived, then we will reign with Him forever. Then Paul wrote the following: "Wherefore, my beloved, as you have always obeyed, not as in my presence only, but now much more in my absence, work out your own salvation with fear and trembling" (Phil. 2:12, KJV) . In other words, be holy and save yourself! Paul commands the saints not to worry about anything, and then he tells us that God will supply all our needs. After Paul finished his letter, he sent it to the saints at Philippi.

During AD 62, Paul was released from his imprisonment in Rome. For the next four years, Paul revisited many of the churches that he established, and he resumed his apostolic ministry as an apostle of Jesus Christ. The church continued to spread and increase in number throughout Africa, Asia, and Europe. It is during this period of time that Paul wrote his first epistle to Timothy.

This letter is considered to be a pastoral epistle because it instructs Christian pastors on how to be godly shepherds of God's elect. Timothy was ministering to the saints at Ephesus during this time. In his letter, Paul warns Timothy against false teachers of the law, and he tells him how men and women should conduct themselves in order to worship God through their lifestyle. Also, Paul tells Timothy that the saints should pray for all authority figures (i.e., kings, presidents). Why, because they're evil and ungodly. We also pray for them so that the church and everyone else will live quiet and peaceful lives in the land. Paul wrote, "For this is good and acceptable in the sight of God our Saviour; who will have all men to be saved, and to come unto the knowledge of the truth. For there is one God, and one Mediator between God and men, the man Christ Jesus" (1 Tim. 2:3–5, KJV). Paul goes on to tell Timothy God's minimum requirements for becoming a bishop and a deacon in the church. Then Paul wrote the following: "And without controversy great is the mystery of godliness: God was manifest (revealed) in the flesh, justified in the Spirit, seen of angels, preached unto the gentiles, believed on in the world, received up into glory" (1 Tim. 3:16, KJV). The God of Israel came in the flesh in order to save humankind from our sins. When Paul finished his letter, he sent it to Timothy.

Soon after Paul wrote to Timothy, he wrote a pastoral epistle to Titus. Titus was ministering to the saints of God on the island of Crete. In his letter, Paul lists all the qualities that a bishop of God must possess. He also tells Titus how to conduct the men and women so that they may live godly lives in this world. Then Paul wrote the following: "For the grace of God that brings salvation has appeared to all men, teaching us that, denying ungodliness and worldly lusts, we should live soberly, righteously, and godly, in this present would; looking for that blessed hope, and the glorious appearing of the great God and our Saviour Jesus Christ" (Titus 2:11–13, KJV). All of God's elect are supposed to be holy and looking forward to Jesus coming back for His church. After Paul finished his letter, he sent it to Titus.

Around AD 63–67, someone wrote an awesome letter to the Jewish Christians. In my opinion, this letter was written by the apostle Paul. I believe this for two reasons: The writing style of this letter is identical to Paul's other epistles, and Paul was one of the few men who had such a great knowledge and revelation of what the Tanakh says concerning the things of God. I may be wrong, but I believe that Paul was the one who wrote the Epistle to the Hebrews. The Hebrew writer begins this letter by writing the following:

> God, after He spoke long ago to the fathers in the prophets in many portions and in many ways, in these last days has spoken to us in His Son, whom He appointed heir of all things, through whom also He made the world. And He is the radiance of His glory and the exact representation of His nature, and upholds all things by the word of His power. When He had made purification of sins, He sat down at the right hand of the Majesty on high. (Heb. 1:1–3, NASB)

Concerning the right hand of God, David K. Bernard wrote the following:

> In the Bible, the right hand signifies strength, power, importance, and pre-eminence just as it does in the English phrases, "He is my right hand man" and "I would give my right arm for this." Trinitarian scholar Bernard Ramm says, "God's almightiness is spoken of in terms of a right arm because among men the right arm is the symbol of strength or power. Pre-eminence is spoken of as sitting at God's right hand because in human social affairs the right hand position with reference to the host was the place of greatest honor."

Jesus the Messiah sits on God's throne in heaven because He is God incarnate. And God has decided to speak to the world through His Son, who is the Word of God.

The teachings that are in this letter are so profound. For instance, the Hebrew writer lets us know that Christ is greater than the prophet Moses and that Melchizedek was an Old Testament type and shadow of Jesus Christ. Also, the Hebrew writer said,

> For this cause He is the Mediator of the New Testament, that by means of death, for the redemption of the transgressions that were under the First Testament, they which are called might receive the promise of eternal inheritance. For where a Testament is, there must also of necessity be the death of the Testator. For a Testament is of force after men are dead: otherwise it is of no strength at all while the Testator lives. Whereupon neither the First Testament was dedicated without blood. (Heb. 9:15–18, KJV)

In other words, Jesus the Anointed One had to die on the cross in order for the church age to begin. This passage of Scripture gives us another explanation for why the thief on the cross was saved without the New Testament form of baptism; he was still under the law of Moses. The Hebrew writer lets us know that if we shrink back into sin, God will not be pleased with us. And if you stay in that position, then you will be lost forever.

The Hebrew writer goes on to say that "faith is the confidence that what we hope for will actually happen; it gives us assurance about things we cannot see" (Heb. 11:1, NLT). After all, we walk by faith, not by sight. Then, he gives us many examples of those before us who lived and died with their faith in God. Lastly, the Hebrew writer tells us that the Lord Jesus never changes. When this letter was finished, it was sent to the Hebrew believers in the Messiah Jesus.

In AD 64, during the reign of Emperor Nero, the city of Rome was set on fire. When the fire began, it burned the city for almost a week. Herbert Benario, professor at Emory University, wrote the following in his online article: "There was brief success in controlling the blaze, but then it burst forth once more, so that many people claimed that the fires were deliberately set." After two more weeks, the fire eventually burned itself out. But the fire was so devastating that it consumed ten of the fourteen Augustan regions in the city. As a result, Nero's popularity decreased dramatically throughout Rome.

For example, Herbert Benario wrote the following: "As his popularity waned, Nero and Tigellinus realized that individuals were needed who could be charged with the disaster. It so happened that there was such a group ready at hand, Christians, who had made themselves unpopular because of their refusal to worship the emperor, their way of life, and their secret meetings."

Nero's attempt to blame the messianic community for the great fire at Rome caused a horrible persecution to breakout against the church. During this period, the churches were fed to wild animals, crucified, and set on fire at night. The church also experienced other grisly forms of executions. So many Christians were martyred in Rome.

Peter was in ancient Mesopotamia ministering to the Jewish saints as their apostle during this horrible time. Also, God inspired Peter to write his first epistle to the saints located in ancient Turkey around AD 64–67.

In his survey of the New Testament, Irving L. Jensen wrote the following:

> The Christians addressed by Peter in this epistle were experiencing fiery trials of their faith (1:6–7). Slander by fellow citizens was one of those trials (2:12). Darker still were the shadows of state persecution, which Christians throughout the Roman Empire feared. Everyone knew about those martyred by Nero in Rome. Would the fires spread to the Christians in northern Asia Minor? Peter wrote this letter not to assure the Christians that persecution would not come, but to encourage them to stand true and endure suffering for Christ's sake and with His strength, even when the persecution grew more intense.

When we go through trials and tribulations, our faith and trust in God should increase to a higher level. These things are designed to transform us into better saints. For example, Peter wrote, "In this you greatly rejoice, though now for a little while you may have had to suffer grief in all kinds of trials. These have come so that your faith—of greater worth than gold, which perishes even though refined by fire—may be proved genuine and may result in praise, glory and honor when Jesus Christ is revealed" (1 Pet. 1:6–8, NIV) . If we maintain our trust in God, then we will receive the goal of our faith, which is the salvation of our souls. Peter goes on to command God's elect to be holy. He also gives explicit commands to all married couples in the faith. Married saints should listen to Peter because God inspired him to write this letter, and Peter was himself a married man.

Peter talked about baptism in his epistle. For example, Peter wrote the following: "God waited patiently in the days of Noah while the ark was being built. In it only a few people, eight in all, were saved through water, and this water symbolizes baptism that now saves you also—not the removal of dirt from the body but the pledge of a good conscience toward God. It saves you by the resurrection of Jesus Christ" (1 Pet. 3:20–21, NIV).

Once again the New Testament clearly states that water baptism is a part of our salvation during the church age. Stop resisting the Holy Ghost and be baptized in the name of Jesus. When Peter finished his letter, he sent it to the churches located in Asia Minor. The messianic community within the Roman Empire continued to suffer persecution and martyrdom throughout the reign of Nero. But despite the emperor's persecution against God's ekklesia, the Lord Jesus continued to strengthen His church daily.

During the years of AD 64–68, God inspired His disciple Mark to write his account of the life of Jesus Christ. It is possible that Mark wrote his version of the good news earlier than this date, but nobody knows for sure. Mark portrays Jesus as the Messiah of God, and the disciple wrote that He healed many people. Also, Mark wrote that the Messiah had brothers. Yet to this day, the Catholics believe that Jesus never had any siblings according to the flesh and that Mary remained a virgin even though she married Joseph. Should we believe the Bible or a large group of lost pagans who constantly disobey God's commands? I'll let you decide for yourself.

Mark wrote that Jesus performed miracles such as calming a storm, feeding five thousand people, and walking on water. Mark also wrote that Jesus said, "For when they shall rise from the dead, they neither marry, nor are given in marriage; but are as the angels which are in Heaven" (Mark 12:25, KJV). Jesus is talking about those who go to heaven after they die. Since we are supposed to take what Jesus said literally, why are so many pastors and evangelists teaching that the fallen angels (demonic spirits) had sexual intercourse with women and produced a race of giants in the book of Genesis? The only difference between an angel and a demon is that one is good and the other is evil; neither of them can procreate with the human race. To all of you who preach this damnable doctrine, repent and embrace the apostle's doctrine!

Mark wrote his version of the death, burial, and resurrection of Jesus the Messiah. At the end of his book, Mark wrote that Jesus said, "Go into all the world and preach the good news to all creation. Whoever believes and is baptized will be saved, but whoever does not believe will be condemned. And these signs will accompany those who believe: In My Name they will drive out demons; they will speak in new tongues; they will pick up snakes with their hands; and when they drink deadly poison, it will not hurt them at all; they will place their hands on sick people, and they will get well." (Mark 16:15–18, NIV). The Lord Himself is saying that you must be baptized in order to be saved. And when a sinner is filled with the Holy Ghost, that person will speak in a new tongue. Repent and receive the grace of God.

And another thing, how dare you so-called scholars continue to this very day to debate the authenticity of Mark 16:9–20. If you read the last chapters of Matthew and Luke, you will plainly see that all three of these gospels say the same thing regarding the events that occurred after

Christ's resurrection from the dead. Why are you people still debating the Gospel of Mark? Let me repeat myself: repent and receive the grace of God according to the Scriptures! Now let's get back to the story.

Around AD 66–67, Paul was arrested and brought to prison in Rome, and he wrote his last letter to Timothy. Six years ago, Paul was imprisoned under pretty comfortable conditions. But this time around, Paul was put in a cold and dark dungeon inside of a Roman prison. But with the help of the Lord Jesus, Paul wrote his second epistle to Timothy. In his letter, Paul encouraged Timothy to remain faithful to Christ and to the work of his ministry. Paul said, "Here is a trustworthy saying: If we died with Him, we will also live with Him; if we endure, we will also reign with Him, if we disown Him, He will also disown us; if we are faithless, He will remain faithful, for He cannot disown Himself" (2 Tim. 2:11–13, NIV). God will remain faithful to us, so we should remain faithful to Jesus and His word. A carnal person would say that Paul had every reason in the world to turn his back on God for allowing him to suffer so much throughout his life. But those of us who are spiritual know that Paul had respect for the recompense of the reward. That reward is eternal life, and Paul was determined to obtain it.

Despite all the things that Paul had went through and his current predicament, the Lord told him that they're lightweight when compared to the times that we are living in right now. For example, Paul wrote the following:

> But mark this: There will be terrible times in the last days. People will be lovers of themselves, lovers of money, boastful, proud, abusive, disobedient to their parents, ungrateful, unholy, without LOVE, unforgiving, slanderous, without self-control, brutal, not lovers of the good, treacherous, rash, conceited, lovers of pleasure rather than lovers of God—having a form of godliness but denying its power. Have nothing to do with them. They are the kind who worm their

> way into homes and gain control over weak-willed women, who are loaded down with sins and are swayed by all kinds of evil desires, *always learning but never able to acknowledge the truth* (2 Tim. 3:1–7, NIV, emphasis mine)

We are living in the last days right now. It is time for the church to wake up and stop playing church and "let us search and examine our ways, and turn back to the Lord" (Lam. 3:40, JPS Bible). And all you people out there who have all the biblical knowledge in the world but can't acknowledge the fact that baptism into the name of Jesus is right, please repent! Lord Jesus, please open up their understanding of what Your holy word says thus.

Prior to finishing his letter, Paul told Timothy, "For I am already being poured out like a drink offering, and the time has come for my departure. I have fought the good fight, I have finished the race, I have kept the faith. Now there is in store for me the crown of righteousness, which the Lord, the righteous Judge, will award to me on that day–and not only to me, but also to all who have longed for His appearing" (2 Tim. 4:6–8, NIV). All saints must continue to fight the good fight of faith and eagerly wait for the return of the Lord Jesus Christ. After he finished writing his letter, Paul sent it to Timothy. For the next six months, Paul suffered while he was in prison. He was tortured almost every day, if not every day, in prison. But Paul never lost his faith in God. He would finally stand trial before Emperor Nero. The emperor sentenced Paul to death. As a result, Paul was led to his executioner, and his head was chopped off. Paul may have greatly suffered throughout his life and ministry, but he died a quick and peaceful death. His death was peaceful because Paul had made his peace with God a long time ago. He is currently in heaven with the rest of the dead in Christ.

During the year AD 67, Peter wrote his second epistle to the saints of God. In his letter, the apostle encourages God's elect to hold on to the promises of God. Then Peter wrote the following: "Knowing this first, that no prophecy of the Scripture is of any private interpretation.

For the prophecy came not in old time by the will of man: but holy men of God spake as they were moved by the Holy Ghost" (2 Pet. 1:20–21, KJV). All true prophecy, which is in the word of God, comes from God and only God. Also, Peter wrote, "Knowing this first, that there shall come in the last days scoffers, walking after their own lusts, and saying, 'Where is the promise of His coming? For since the fathers fell asleep, all things continue as they were from the beginning of the creation (2 Pet. 3:3–4, KJV).'" It's obvious that so many people in the world knows about the rapture because I have never seen so many sinners mock and make fun of it. The Lord Jesus is doing His part to save souls, but they're rejecting God's great salvation. The world is without excuse.

Prior to finishing his letter, Peter wrote the following: "Bear in mind that our Lord's patience means salvation, just as our dear brother Paul also wrote you with the wisdom that God gave him. He writes the same way in all his letters, speaking in them of these matters. His letters contain some things that are hard to understand, which ignorant and unstable people distort, as they do the other Scriptures, to their own destruction" (2 Pet. 3:15–16, NIV). Now, I know that the New Testament scriptures are hard to understand, but that doesn't give us the excuse whatsoever to preach and/ or teach false doctrines because of our lack of understanding. If you don't humble yourself and ask God to open up your understanding of what it takes to obtain eternal life, then you will not only distort every other portion of the Scriptures, you'll also reject sound doctrine. This is true in today's world. For example, I once read an online article in which a preacher said, "I would rather obey the words of Jesus than the words of Peter." What! Has that preacher ever read the Gospel according to Luke? Maybe he did read Luke's gospel, but he didn't understand Jesus when He said, "He who hears you hears Me." In fact, Jesus Himself gave Peter the keys to the kingdom of heaven. So the words of Yeshua and Peter are in harmony.

After Peter finished his letter, he sent it to the churches that he was addressing at that time. Sometime later, Peter was captured, brought to Rome, and crucified on an X-shaped cross. The reason why Peter died this way is he thought that he was unworthy to die the same way that the Messiah died, so he was crucified upside-down on an X-shaped cross. Nobody knows for sure, but Peter's wife and children were probably martyred as well. Peter is currently in heaven with the rest of the dead in Christ.

During AD 66–70, the Jewish Zealots led the Great Revolt against the Roman Empire. The Jews rebelled against Rome for a number of reasons. According to Solomon Zeitlin, "The combination of financial exploitation, Rome's unbridled contempt for Judaism, and the unabashed favoritism that the Romans extended to gentiles living in Israel brought about the revolt." It began when Florus, the last Roman procurator, stole vast quantities of silver from the second temple of King Solomon. After this happened, the Jews rioted and killed the Roman garrison that was stationed in Jerusalem. The Romansresponded when Cestius Gallus, the Roman ruler in Syria, sent a larger force of soldiers to Jerusalem. Those soldiers were also defeated by the Zealots. When this happened, the number of Jewish Zealots increased because they thought that their victories against the Romans meant that God was on their side. Unfortunately, they were so wrong.

The Romans returned to Judea with sixty thousand heavily armed and highly trained troops. They attacked and utterly destroyed the Zealots who were in Galilee. About one hundred thousand Jews were killed or sold into slavery by the Romans. Solomon Zeitlin wrote the following in his online article:

> Throughout the Roman conquest of this territory, the Jewish leadership in Jerusalem did almost nothing to help their beleaguered brothers. They apparently had concluded—too late, unfortunately—that the revolt could not be won, and wanted to hold down Jewish deaths as much as possible. The highly embittered refugees who succeeded in escaping the Galilean massacres fled to the last major Jewish stronghold

Jerusalem. There, they killed anyone in the Jewish leadership who was not as radical as they. Thus, all the more moderate Jewish leaders who headed the Jewish government at the revolt's beginning in 66 were dead by 68—and not one died at the hands of a Roman. All were killed by fellow Jews.

It was obvious that the Jews were not going to defeat the Romans, but they did not make it easier on themselves by engaging in a suicidal civil war. In AD 68, Emperor Nero killed himself by stabbing himself in the neck. I think we all know where he is right now.

Eighteen months later, Titus Flavius Vespasianus (AD 69–79) became the emperor of the Roman Empire. He restored peace and stability to an empire left in disorder following the death of Nero. The Roman Empire may have been restored, but the churches were in disarray as they were being scattered and hunted like wild animals. And due to the ongoing chaos in Jerusalem, the messianic community vacated that city. So in AD 70, General Titus (the emperor's son) and his army breached the walls of Jerusalem and initiated an orgy of violence and destruction. The city of Jerusalem, including the second temple of King Solomon, the son of David, was utterly destroyed. Only the valuable artifacts that were in the temple survived.

It is estimated that one million Jews died in the Great Revolt against Rome. Men, women, and children were brutally killed. And a great number of Jews were sold into slavery. Also, the destruction of the Jewish temple put an immediate end to the Jewish practice of animal sacrifices. In addition, the Zealots that were able to escape the Romans in Jerusalem were eventually hunted down and killed. This marks the beginning of the Jews' exile from their holy land, and this horrible event caused the scattering of the Jews throughout the whole world. By the grace of God, the Jews were able to continue to live their lives within the empire. But for the next three centuries, anyone who was found practicing the teachings of Christ was brutally killed, especially if that saint refused to deny his or her faith in Jesus. And any Jew who tried to cause any more trouble against the Roman Empire was killed as well. So the church went underground in order to spread, but the survival of the faith within the empire was in total danger of being wiped out by Satan.

During the chaos of the Great Revolt, Jude, another younger half brother of Christ Jesus, wrote his epistle to the saints of God around AD 67–68. Some scholars believe that he wrote his letter at a later date, but nobody knows for sure. In his letter, Jude said,

> Dear friends, although I was very eager to write to you about the salvation we share, I felt I had to write and urge you to contend for the faith that was once for all entrusted to the saints. For certain men whose condemnation was written about long ago have secretly slipped in among you. They are godless men, who change the grace of our God into a license for immorality and deny Jesus Christ our only Sovereign and Lord. (Jude 1:3–4, NIV)

It appears that some false brethren had infiltrated the ekklesia and started to teach false doctrines, which deceived the saints and caused some of us to sin against Jesus. Marvin M. Arnold wrote the following in his outline to describe these men:

> Most were apostate Greeks who had been seethed in Platonism, polytheism, mythology and philosophy. Some could never understand monotheism as in Deuteronomy 6:4. Saint Matthew 24:24 had foretold the arising of false clerics.

We are supposed to know what the Bible says for ourselves so that when false brethren try to come in among us and pervert the word of God, we won't be deceived by their damnable heresies.

In the same epistle, Jude wrote,

> Enoch, the seventh from Adam, prophesied about these men: "See, the Lord is coming with thousands upon thousands

of His holy ones to judge everyone, and to convict all the ungodly of all the ungodly acts they have done in the ungodly way, and of all the harsh words ungodly sinners have spoken against Him." (Jude 1:14–15, NIV)

If these men and everyone else in the world don't repent of their sins and get saved, they will be sent to the lake of fire!

Also, Jude wrote,

> But you, beloved, building up yourselves on your most holy faith, praying in the Holy Ghost, keep yourselves in the love of God, looking for the mercy of our Lord Jesus Christ unto eternal life. And on some have compassion, making a difference: and others save with fear, pulling them out of the fire; hating even the garment spotted by the flesh. (Jude 1:20–23, KJV)

You heard the man saints; we are supposed to keep on speaking in other tongues because this is our spiritual method of edifying ourselves. And we have to use wisdom when we're witnessing to lost souls, for he who wins souls is wise. Jude also lets us know that our God is able to keep His churches from slipping and falling back into sin; all we have to do is use our Holy Ghost power to be holy. Jude finished writing this God-breathed letter and sent it to the churches that he was addressing. He continued to work with the saints of God to make disciples out of sinners till he died.

Since the year AD 44, the churches of God, including the apostles and disciples of Christ, were being persecuted and brutally martyred throughout the known world. God was still using His saints to save sinners, but the ekklesia faced the possibility of death every day of their lives. According to *Foxe's Book of Martyrs*, the Apostle Philip was in Phrygia preaching the gospel of God. While Philip was at Hierapolis, he was scourged and afterward crucified in AD 54. Matthew was in Ethiopia when he was killed by a sword wound. Mark was in Alexandria,

Egypt, when he was killed; they tied him to horses and dragged his body through the streets until he was dead. According to Grant Jeffrey, the Apostle Bartholomew was in ancient Armenia when he was killed. Bartholomew was flayed to death by a whip. James, the other apostle, was thrown over a hundred feet down from the southeast pinnacle of the temple when he refused to deny his faith in Jesus. Somehow, he survived the fall. So when his killers realized that he was still alive, they severely beat him with a fuller's club and crushed his skull.

The apostle Andrew was whipped severely by seven different Roman soldiers in ancient Greece. Afterward, they crucified him on an X-shaped cross and tied his body to the cross with cords in order to prolong his agony. According to tradition, he preached to the people that were looking at him on the cross for about two days. *Two days!* By the grace of God, Andrew finally died and went up into glory. In my opinion, the apostle Paul suffered the most throughout his life, but Andrew died the worst death out of all the apostles. The way Andrew died teaches the church that no matter what man does to us, it is nothing when compared to the torments of hell. Also, the Lord Jesus is able to keep us from falling even while dying in agony.

Matthias, the one chosen to replace Judas Iscariot, was stoned and then beheaded. Thomas was stabbed and killed with a spear in ancient India. Thaddaeus (a.k.a. Judas) was killed by being shot with arrows. Another source does state that Judas was crucified, but the former is the popular belief. Barnabas was stoned to death at Salonica. And Simon the Zealot was crucified around AD 74. The Romans crucified both men and women, and who knows what they did to the children with their sick and twisted minds. Also, they took the churches to high places and threw the saints off them. The Romans took pride in using their imagination to come up with all kinds of ways of destroying God's ekklesia. John the apostle was the only one of the original eleven who was still alive.

Around AD 85, while the emissary John was living in the city of Ephesus, God inspired him to write his account of the life of Jesus the Messiah. John gives us his version of what occurred when Jesus approached the prophet John the Baptizer at the Jordan River. For example, John wrote the following:

> The next day John sees Jesus coming unto him, and says, "Behold the Lamb of God, which takes away the sin of the world. This is He of whom I said, 'After me comes a Man which is preferred before me: for He was before me. And I knew Him not: but that He should be made manifest to Israel, therefore am I come baptizing with water.'" And John bare record, saying, "I saw the Spirit descending from Heaven like a dove, and it abode upon Him. And I knew Him not: but He that sent me to baptize with water, the same said unto me, 'Upon whom you shalt see the Spirit descending, and remaining on Him, the same is He which baptizes with the Holy Ghost.' And I saw, and bare record that this is the Son of God." Again the next day after John stood, and two of his disciples; and looking upon Jesus as He walked, he said, "Behold the Lamb of God!" (John 1:29–36, KJV)

This passage of Scripture speaks for itself. Jesus was baptized at the Jordan River so that God could show the people of Israel that the Messiah has come. The baptism of Jesus, which is also recorded in the other gospels, is not an example of the Trinity in action. The Holy Ghost, who is God the Father, manifested Himself as a dove and descended on the Messiah so that Israel could see that Jesus is the Anointed One. This is how Jesus's ministry began. Please repent and embrace the oneness of God.

John wrote about the things that Jesus said and did during His ministry. For instance, John wrote that Jesus told a Pharisee that he must be born again. This command applies to all sinners. Also, Jesus made the following statement: "For God so loved the world, that He gave His only begotten Son, that whosoever believes in Him should not perish, but have everlasting life" (John 3:16, KJV). Whoever believes in Jesus, gets baptized in the name of Jesus and is immersed in the Holy Ghost will have eternal life! I am telling you what the Scriptures mean because I love you, so humble yourself and embrace the truth. John wrote that Jesus told a woman that God is a Spirit. The Messiah knows this to be true because He is that Spirit incarnate. Then John wrote about Jesus going to the Feast of Tabernacles to teach the Jews His doctrine. The Jews were so amazed at His teaching that they asked Jesus how He learned it. John wrote that Jesus said, "My doctrine is not Mine, but His that sent Me" (John 7:16). The doctrine of Christ is the doctrine of God.

Jesus testified of His deity on several occasions. For example, John wrote that the Lord said, "And he that sees Me sees Him that sent Me" (John 12:45) and "He that has seen Me has seen the Father" (John 14:9). During the Last Supper, Jesus tells His disciples about the Holy Ghost. Jesus said, "If you love Me, keep My commandments. And I will pray the Father, and He shall give you another Comforter, that He may abide with you forever; even the Spirit of truth; whom the world cannot receive, because it sees Him not, neither knows Him: but you know Him; for He dwells with you, and shall be in you. I will not leave you comfortless: I will come to you" (John 14:15–18). Jesus Christ was either both insane and suffering from multiple personality disorder, or He is what He said He is: The Holy Spirit our Father manifested in the flesh as the Son of God.

Here is another passage of Scripture that is confusing to the Christian world: The Son of Man praying to God the Father. John wrote that Jesus said, "Father, glorify Me in Your presence with the glory I had with You before the world began. I have revealed Your Name to those whom You gave Me out of the world. They were Yours; You gave them to Me and they have obeyed Your word" (John 17:5–6, NIV). Jesus also said, "Holy Father, protect them by the power of Your Name—the Name You gave Me—so that they may be one as We are one. While I was with them, I protected them and kept them safe by that Name You gave Me" (John 17:11–12, NIV). Jesus finished His prayer by saying, "O righteous Father, the world has not known You: but I have known You, and these have known that You have sent Me. And I have declared unto them Your Name, and will declare it: that the love wherewith You have loved Me may be in them, and I in them" (John 17:25–26, KJV).

What you are seeing here, as well as in the other gospels of Jesus, is an example of the human side of Christ praying to the God of Israel who is also in Him. The Son of Man prayed to God in order to accomplish His will and to give the church a perfect example of how the relationship between God and a saint should be. And when the Son of God prays for us, you can be sure that His prayers will be answered by God.

The apostle went on to write his version of the death, burial, and resurrection of Jesus the Messiah. Then John concluded his book by writing his account of what Jesus did after His resurrection. After he finished his book, John shared it with the churches of God.

The four gospels of Christ have been written so that the church would have the complete story of the earthly life of Jesus.

The apostle John wrote three God-breathed epistles to the church around AD 85–90. In his first letter, John wrote the following:

> If we say that we have not sinned, we make Him a liar, and His word is not in us. My little children, these things write I unto you, that you sin not. And if any man sin, we have an advocate [*paracletos*] with the Father, Jesus Christ the Righteous: and He is the propitiation for our sins: and not for ours only, but also for the sins of the whole world. (1 John 1:10–2:2, KJV)

When a saint was baptized in the name of Jesus and filled with the Spirit of Christ, the strength and power of his/her sinful nature has been destroyed forever. A saint still has his/ her sinful nature, but the flesh no longer has any power over the church. King Solomon wrote, "For there is not one good man on earth who does what is best and doesn't err" (Eccles. 7:20, JPS Bible). None of us are infallible, but we don't have to sin against God. John wrote this letter to the saints to let us know that we don't have to continue to sin because of the Holy Ghost, which Jesus has given us.

In the same letter, John commands the church not to love the world or anything in it. Why? Because Lucifer is the god of this world; the world is completely subject to him. If you love the world, then the love of God isn't in you.

> The one who practices sin is of the devil; for the devil has sinned from the beginning. (1 John 3:8, NASB)

> Dear children, let us not love with words or tongue but with actions and in truth. (1 John 3:18, NIV)

Whoa! These are some cold Scriptures, but we must live by them. In addition, the apostle commands us to love one another. Then John wrote, "This is the One who came by water and blood—Jesus Christ. He did not come by water only, but by water and blood, and it is the Spirit who testifies, because the Spirit is the truth. For there are three that testify: the Spirit, the water and the blood; and the three are in agreement" (1 John 5:6–8, NIV). John is telling us that the water, the name of Jesus (where the blood is), and the baptism of the Holy Spirit constitutes one baptism. In other words, these three agree in one just as God is one. This is the reason why God inspired Paul to write the fact that there's one Lord and one baptism. Lastly, John concluded his first letter by commanding the saints of God to keep ourselves from idols.

Sometime later, the emissary wrote a second letter to the ekklesia. John wrote the following: "For many deceivers are entered into the world, who confess not that Jesus Christ is come in the flesh. This is a deceiver and an antichrist. Look to yourselves, that we lose not those things which we have wrought, but that we receive a full reward. Whosoever transgresses, and abides not in the doctrine of Christ, has not God. He that abides in the doctrine of Christ, he has both the Father and the Son" (2 John 1:7–9, KJV). The apostle's doctrine is the doctrine of Christ, and the doctrine of the Messiah is the doctrine of God. If you don't embrace this teaching, you will be eternally damned! I am only repeating what the Scriptures teach.

Soon after the apostle finished his second letter, John wrote his third letter to the messianic community. John also addressed his letter to Gaius, his brother in Christ. John wrote, "Dear friend, do not imitate what is evil but what is good. Anyone who does what is good is from God. Anyone who does what is evil has not seen God" (3 John 1:11, NIV). I hope you noticed that all the epistles in the New Testament commands the church to be holy. Christianity is a way of life, and this life is peaceful because our peace comes from God. After John wrote all of these God-breathed epistles, he shared them with the saints of *El Shaddai* (God Almighty). And the apostle's doctrine continued to spread throughout the known world.

Now Emperor Domitian ruled the Roman Empire during the years of AD 8 1–96. Domitian ruled in an almost tyrannical reign of terror in which many perished, including Christians. And around AD 95–96, the apostle John was caught in a wave of persecution while still residing in Asia Minor. Even though John was over ninety years old, he continued to preach the gospel of Jesus and teach the doctrine of the Messiah. Since John refused to stop preaching in the name of Jesus, the Romans tried to kill the apostle by throwing him into a huge basin of boiling oil. After John was thrown into the basin, something happened that wasn't supposed to happen: the apostle was still alive! And everybody who was there saw it with their own eyes. John miraculously survived the ordeal because it wasn't in the will of God for the apostle to die in this way. Since the Romans were unable to kill the apostle, they banished John to an island called Patmos in order to silence him from preaching the good news. At that time, Patmos was a quarry mine for political prisoners, criminals, and slaves. Shortly after John was banished to Patmos, Emperor Domitian was brutally stabbed to death. Most Christian scholars believe that Domitian was the one who ordered the banishment of John to Patmos. Once again, nobody messes with God's anointed ones and gets away with it. John may have suffered as a criminal, but it was in the will of God for the apostle to be at Patmos. The Lord Jesus was with him, and according to the apostle Paul, "God causes all things to work together for good to those who love God, to those who are called according to His purpose" (Rom. 8:28, NASB).

Around AD 96–97, the Lord Jesus Christ appeared to the apostle John and inspired him to write the book of Revelation. This book gives the church a deeper revelation of who Jesus the Messiah is, and it tells us about the fulfillment of the prophet Daniel's last seven (the seven-year tribulation). John wrote that he was in the Spirit when Christ revealed to him that He is the First and the Last and He holds the keys of death and hell. The devil doesn't even have the keys to his own kingdom. Also, the Lord commanded John to write to the seven churches, which are located in ancient Turkey. Two of these churches, which are located in Smyrna and Philadelphia, were in the will of God. But the churches that are located in Ephesus, Pergamum, Thyatira, Sardis, and Laodicea were not in the will of God. The problems that were occurring in these churches will be the same problems that will occur in God's ekklesia all throughout church history. After all, King Solomon wrote, "Only that shall happen which has happened, only that occur which has occurred; there is nothing new beneath the sun!" (Eccles. 1:9, JPS Bible). The saints of God are not infallible, but we are doing the best we can to love and serve God according to the Scriptures.

God commanded His five churches to repent of their deeds, and then Jesus showed John awesome visions of what would happen in the future. John wrote, "After this I looked, and, behold, a door was opened in heaven: and the first voice which I heard was as it were of a trumpet talking with me; which said, 'Come up here, and I will show you things which must be hereafter.' And immediately I was in the Spirit; and, behold, a throne was set in heaven, and One sat on the throne" (Rev. 4:1–2, kjv). John saw a vision of the Lord Jesus sitting on His throne. John also saw twenty-four elders and four beasts surrounding God's throne. These elders and beasts represent God's original and primitive ekklesia; everything that God was showing John is real and symbolic. The church will remain in heaven until we come back to earth with the Lord. Then John saw the Lord Jesus holding a scroll in His hand. The scroll had been sealed with seven seals, and nobody was able to open the scroll except for the Lamb of God. John saw Jesus in all His deity on the throne and in His humanity as the Lamb slain. David K. Bernard wrote the following:

> Revelation 4:2 and 8 describe the One on the throne as the "Lord God Almighty, which was, and is, and is to come." Yet, in Revelation 1:8 Jesus describes Himself as "the Lord, which is, and which was, and which is to come, the Almighty." (See 1:11–18 and 22:12–16 for further proof that Jesus is the speaker of 1:8.) Also the One on the throne is the Judge (Revelation 20:11–12), and we know that Jesus will be the Judge of all (John 5:22, 27; Romans 2:16; 14:10–11). Therefore, we can conclude that the One on the throne is Jesus in all His power and Deity.

David K. Bernard continues his point by writing the following:

> The Lamb is the Son of God—Jesus Christ in His humanity, particularly in His sacrificial role. The New Testament identifies Jesus as the Lamb who offered His blood for our sins (John 1:36; I Peter 1:19) . That is why Revelation 5:6 describes the Lamb as slain. God could not and did not die; only the humanity of Jesus died. So the Lamb represents Jesus

> only in His humanity as a sacrifice for sin. The rest of chapter 5 also proves this by describing the Lamb as our Redeemer.

Once again, the New Testament teaches us the oneness of God and the dual nature of Jesus the Messiah. When the Lamb opened the first four seals, John saw a man riding a white horse, a red horse, a black horse, and a pale horse. The four horsemen are four different representations of the same man who will become the leader of the future one world government. He is called the Antichrist because he is against the Jewish Messiah. The New World Order will officially take place after the rapture of God's church and during the seven-year tribulation period.

After the man of sin was revealed, John recorded that God chose and sealed 144,000 Jews from the twelve tribes of Israel. Jesus also sent two witnesses into the earth to preach and prophesy. They were the same two olive trees that the prophet Zechariah saw; they were anointed to serve the Lord of all the earth. This happened during the first forty-two months of the tribulation. In the midst of their preaching, John wrote that God poured out His wrath on the inhabitants of the earth. It was estimated that half of the world's population would be killed during the first forty-two months of Daniel's last seven-year period. After the two witnesses finished giving their testimony to the world, the Antichrist overpowered and killed them at Jerusalem. But after three and a half days, God brought them back to life and received them up into heaven. In addition to all of this, John recorded that the Antichrist would introduce the mark of the beast to the human race. John wrote,

> And he causes all, the small and the great, and the rich and the poor, and the free men and the slaves, to be given a mark on their right hand, or on their forehead, and he provides that no one should be able to buy or to sell, except the one who has the mark, either the name of the beast or the number of his name. Here is wisdom. Let him who has

understanding calculate the number of the beast, for the number is that of a man; and his number is six hundred and sixty-six. (Rev. 13:16–18, NASB)

Woe to everybody who is alive during this time of the tribulation. In order to make it into heaven, you must be willing to die for the name of Jesus. And if you're not willing to get saved and spiritually die to your old self during this dispensation, then what makes you think that you will be able to physically die for Christ during the New World Order?

Everyone who dies during Daniel's last seven years for the name of Jesus are tribulation saints. After the last soul was killed because of his or her refusal to take the mark of the beast, God continued to pour out His wrath upon the earth until the seven years were over. Then John saw the Lord Jesus and His heavenly army come down to earth to destroy the Antichrist and his army during the battle at Armageddon. The Lord saved the Jews who survived the worst seven years of earth's history, put the devil in the bottomless pit, and established His millennial kingdom on earth. This was the kingdom that the prophet Isaiah prophesied during his ministry. After the one thousand years of peace are over, Satan was released from his prison and he gathered men from all over the globe to Jerusalem. This was the last battle between God and the devil. The Lord Jesus rained fire on Lucifer and his followers, and He tossed Satan into the lake of fire forever. Thank you, Lord Jesus!

John went on to record what occurred at the great white throne judgment of God. Everyone who ever lived was brought back to life and judged according to their deeds while they lived. Anyone's name that was not found in the book of life was hurled into the lake of fire forever! Lastly, John described the new heaven and earth, and he ended this great book by writing the following: "He which testifies these things saith, 'Surely I come quickly.' Amen. Even so, come, Lord Jesus. The grace of our Lord Jesus Christ be with you all. Amen" (Rev. 22:20–21, KJV) . The books of the Holy Bible, which include the *Tanakh* and the *Brit Hadashah* (New Covenant), are now complete.

Before I move on with the story of John's life, I must share with you another dream that God gave me during the fall of 2008. I did not see the golden city of New Jerusalem, but God did show me certain parts of the new heaven and earth. Everything that I saw was real and symbolic. This is the dream that God gave me: I was looking outside of a window, and I saw the sky and a river of water. The water that I saw was clear as crystal; I have never seen water like the river that I saw. The water was perfectly blue, and it had no impurities or pollution in it. I looked down the window, and I noticed that I was in a huge boat or ship, and it was in the middle of the river. The river was perfectly blue at close range as well as from a distance. There were no clouds in the sky. In fact, it was bright outside, but there was no sun giving its light to the earth. As I went back inside of the ship, I noticed that the inside of the ship looked just like the sanctuary of the house of God that I attend: Peace Apostolic Church. Everything that is in the sanctuary of my church was there except for the pews, the pulpit, the chandeliers, and the chairs where the choir sits. I saw some of the saints that attend my church, and they were sitting on the floor.

I saw my pastor and some of the ministers under him sitting on the steps close to where the pulpit was supposed to be. Also, there were a few angels inside the sanctuary. They were just standing the left of the sanctuary and watching the saints. The saints of God were having a conversation with the pastor, and he was doing most of the talking. He was talking to the saints about the things of God and how we made it into the new heaven and earth. All the saints had our gloried bodies. I know this because after the saints finished talking to the pastor, we jumped through the walls of the ship and went for a swim in the water. I literally saw the saints, including myself, go through the walls of the ship and into the water. The saints were in the river for at most a moment. Then the saints jumped out of the water. The very second that the saints, including myself, jumped out of the water, we were immediately dry, and we went back into the ship by going through it.

Once the saints were back inside the ship, I saw the ship from the outside heading toward land. The ship was a gigantic ark made out of gopher wood. In fact, based on what I saw, the ark was slightly bigger than the replica ark that was built in the Netherlands by Johan Huibers several years ago. The ark was sailing on the river all by itself. In other words, the Spirit of the Lord was driving it. Once the ark reached land, a door at the side of the ark opened by itself. Then, I went to the upper part inside of the ark and looked at the land through a window. The land looked nothing like the land that currently exists on earth; it was completely brand new, and it had no corruption in it. And I saw some more saints who attend my church walking on the land and coming inside of the ark. This was how my dream ended.

Two days after I had this dream, the Lord Jesus revealed to me the meaning of the things that I saw in my dream. The meaning of the things that I saw are the following: The water that the ark was on is the river of the water of life, which flows from the throne of God and of the Lamb. The land is the new earth. The angels are the ministering spirits who serve those who will inherit eternal life, and they encamp round about and protect God's ekklesia from the evil one. The light that lighted the whole earth was God's *Sh'khinah*. Jesus the Messiah is God's revealed *Sh'khinah*! And the ark itself represents the house of God where the saints meet together in order to encourage one another, fellowship, and hear the pastor preach the message of salvation. Also, the ark represents a place of safety. For example, when Noah and his family entered into the ark, Yeshua shut the door and flooded the earth with water. Everyone who was not in the ark was killed by the water, but Noah and his family were saved through that same water because they were inside the ark. The ark was a safe haven for them.

The saints of God are safe in the Messiah because the name of Jesus is their strong tower! As I mentioned earlier, my pastor was talking to the saints about how we made it into the new heaven and earth. The saints of God know that the gospel of Christ, water baptism in the name of Jesus, being filled with the Holy Ghost, growing in our salvation, walking in kingdom authority, and living a holy lifestyle are the reasons why we're going to the new heaven. But how would my pastor know about salvation unless God revealed it to him? And how would the saints who attend my church know what the pastor knows unless he preaches the good news of Christ? As it is written, "Faith comes by hearing, and hearing by the word of God." We are going to the new heaven and earth because we preach the gospel of Jesus and teach the doctrine of Christ according to the Scriptures. These are the reasons why my church is a place of safety. Peace Apostolic Church is an ark of safety. Not just my church, but every apostolic center in this world that teaches the doctrine of Christ and preaches the oneness of God. So if you go to a church whose pastor, whether male or female, is sent by God to preach Jesus, then your house of worship is an ark of safety. Jesus Christ is our ark of safety! Now that the saints have eternal life, be ye holy for our God is holy.

After two years of imprisonment, the apostle John was released from the isle of Patmos. This happened either during the reign of Emperor Nerva (AD 96–98) or Trajan (AD 98–117). Most biblical scholars, including Irving L. Jensen, believe that the apostle went back to Ephesus and lived there throughout the rest of his days. But prior to his return to Asia Minor, Timothy suffered martyrdom in Ephesus. John continued to preach the gospel of Jesus and teach the doctrine of the Messiah. As a result, many souls were baptized in the name of Jesus Christ, and God gave them the gift of the Holy Ghost. Also, the apostle shared the book of Revelation with the churches and taught the saints what the Lord Jesus had revealed to him. The church lived their lives as if the Lord Jesus was soon to return for His messianic community. And around AD 99–100, the apostle John died a peaceful death as an old man. He is currently in heaven with the dead in Christ.

God's ekklesia continued to spread throughout the ancient nations of Africa, Asia, and Europe. But within the Roman Empire, the church was troubled on every side, yet not distressed. The saints were perplexed, but not in despair; persecuted, but not forsaken by God; we were cast down by our enemies, but not destroyed by them. With the Lord Jesus dwelling inside of His saints, God's original and primitive ekklesia marched triumphantly into the second century.

THE SECOND CENTURY

The original and primitive ekklesia entered into the post-apostolic age. In fact, this period of time began during the later years of the apostle John, and it lasted during the years of AD 90–140. The most prominent leaders of the church were Clement of Rome, Hermas, Polycarp, and Ignatius of Antioch. All of these men preached the gospel of Jesus and taught the doctrine of Christ. And according to the New Testament, Clement was a fellow worker of the apostle Paul during his ministry. It is believed that both Ignatius and Polycarp were disciples of the apostle John.

Clement wrote two letters to the churches that teach the fundamental principles of the apostle's doctrine. For instance, his first was addressed to the saints who were at Rome and Corinth. In his first letter, Clement wrote the following: "The Apostles received for us the gospel from our Lord Jesus Christ; our Lord Jesus Christ received it from God. Christ, therefore, was sent out from God, and the Apostles from Christ; and both these things were done in good order, according to the will of God." Clement also wrote, "Have we not one God and one Christ? Is not the Spirit of grace, which was poured out upon us, one? Is not our calling one in Christ?" This sounds like biblical teaching to me. And in his second letter, Clement wrote, "If we say that...the Spirit is Christ, then he who does violence to the Church does violence to Christ. Such a man will not share in the Spirit, which is the Christ." Notice how Clement calls the Spirit "Christ." This same Spirit is the Holy Spirit which Paul said is "Christ in you, the hope of glory." Clement served the Lord until he was martyred around AD 100.

Now Trajan was the emperor of the Roman Empire. During his reign, Pliny was the governor of Bithynia -Pontus (ancient northern Turkey). In this period, the emperor forbade meetings of secret societies in order to hinder their potential of overthrowing the authority of the empire by influencing the people; Christians were included in this group. But despite his feelings toward secret societies in general, Trajan was pretty tolerant of the church. It was Governor Pliny who was weary of the spread of Christianity. Samson Hutagalung wrote the following in his online article:

> He condemned Christianity to be practiced in Bithynia. But the rapid growth of Christianity had caused him to send the letter to the emperor for further instruction. The main reason of Pliny for executing judgement to Christians was because he understood that Christians had caused the temple of their gods to have no business. As Pliny wrote to Trajan "that this superstition was constantly spreading, not only in the cities, but also in the villages of Asia Minor, and captivated people of every age, rank, and sex, so that the temples were almost forsaken, and the sacrificial victims found no sale."

The Holy Ghost was falling like rain in Bithynia. But due to Pliny's hatred towards the messianic community, many saints suffered martyrdom. In fact, Trajan replied to Pliny's letter by telling him that he was doing the right thing by punishing Christians without his consent. The emperor also told Pliny that if anyone was brought to him on suspicion of being a Christian and refused to renounce Christ, then that person must be executed. But if that person renounced Jesus and offered prayers to the Roman gods, then that person will be pardoned and set free.

No true Christian denied Christ before Pliny nor offered supplications to the gods of Rome. In fact, Pliny said, "Real Christians (I understand) can never be induced to do these things." And according to Samson Hutagalung, the following event occurred in Antioch, Syria:

> Trajan came to Antioch and threatened to persecute those who refused to offer sacrifice to their gods. The man of God by the name of Ignatius, who lived in those days, proudly confessed that he was a bearer of God and he was not afraid of Trajan. Ignatius said that he had Christ within his breast. For this reason Ignatius was condemned by Trajan and thrown to the lions in Rome.

Nobody knows for sure when these events occurred. All of these things, including Ignatius's death, probably occurred in the year AD 107 (if not later). The persecution of the saints continued throughout Trajan's reign. But the ekklesia, through the leadership and strength of the Holy Ghost, continued to increase in number throughout the empire.

Prior to his death, Ignatius was the bishop of the church in Antioch. Most sources state that he was born in AD 35. Very little is known about his life. But it is a fact that he came in contact with the church, was baptized in the name of Jesus Christ, and was filled with the Holy Ghost during the first century. Also, we know that Ignatius wrote many letters to the saints throughout the Roman Empire. But we only have six of his letters that are considered to be authentic. His letters are the epistles he wrote to the Ephesians, Magnesians, Trallians, Romans, Philadelphians, and Smyrnaeans. In his letter to the Ephesians, Ignatius taught that Jesus Christ is the Holy Ghost. Also, Ignatius's letters to the Smyrnaeans and Trallians reflect the dilemma of the ekklesia during his latter years. John the apostle had passed away, centrifugal forces were at work, differences of theological opinion were arising, and churches had a tendency to split up into sections. So Ignatius tried to resolve each problem through his epistles because the unity of the church in Asia Minor was in danger. NNDB's online article on Ignatius of Antioch states the following:

> The only remedy for it in those days was to exalt the authority of the ministry and make it the center of church life. It should be noted that (1) there is no trace of the later doctrine of apostolical succession; (2) the ministry is never sacerdotal in the letters of Ignatius. As Lightfoot puts it: "The ecclesiastical order was enforced by him (Ignatius) almost solely as a security for doctrinal purity. The threefold ministry was the husk, the shell, which protected the precious kernel of the truth."

In other words, Ignatius exalted the God-given authority of the bishops, presbyters, and deacons of the ekklesia to keep the saints in the will of God. Ignatius was not a Nicolaitan with a takeover spirit in the church. He never wanted to elevate men above God. He just wanted the saints to contend for the apostle's doctrine and stay in Christ. After all, Hebrews 13:17 says, "Obey them that have the rule over you, and submit yourselves: for they watch for your souls, as they that must give account, that they may do it with joy, and not with grief: for that is unprofitable for you." Ignatius's letters are his legacy in the church of God.

After the death of Emperor Trajan, Hadrian (AD 117–138) ascended to the throne. During his reign, Hermas wrote the *Shepherd of Hermas* around AD 120. Nobody knows for sure when he was converted, but he was baptized in the name of Jesus Christ, and God filled him with the Holy Ghost. Also, Hermas had embraced the oneness of God according to the Scriptures. For instance, Hermas wrote, "After I had written down the commandments and parables of the shepherd, the angel of repentance, he came to me and saith to me; 'I wish to show you all things that the Holy Spirit, which spake with you in the form of the Church, showed unto you. For that Spirit is the Son of God.'" Hermas is saying that the Son of God is the Holy Spirit incarnate. This is what the New Testament teaches. Hermas also wrote the following:

> "It was necessary for them," says he, "to rise up through water, that they might be made alive; for otherwise they could not enter into the kingdom of God, except they had put aside the deadness of their [former] life. So these likewise that had fallen asleep received the seal of the Son of God and entered into the kingdom of God. For before a man," says he, "has borne the name of [the Son of] God, he is dead; but when he has received the seal, he lays aside his deadness, and resumes life. The seal then is the water: so they go down into the water dead, and they come up alive. Thus to them also this seal was preached, and they availed themselves of it that they might enter into the kingdom of God."

Now he is talking about water baptism into the name of Jesus the Messiah. Hermas also wrote about so many other things in his letter that pertains to holiness and the oneness of God. He did this by quoting Scriptures from the Holy Bible. He obviously had his own copies of the Holy Scriptures in writing. So after Hermas finished his letter, his writings were accepted by many of the ancient church leaders and read routinely in the church. Why? Because his writings edified the teachings of the New Testament.

In the beginning of Hadrian's reign, he was sympathetic toward the Jews. In fact, he allowed the Israelites to return to Jerusalem and rebuild the holy temple in AD 118. But as the Jews were making preparations to rebuild the third temple, the emperor quickly went back on his word. Also, he began deporting Jews to North Africa. As a result, the

Jews devised plans to seek vengeance against the Roman Empire. Shira Schoenberg wrote the following in his online article:

> The Jews organized guerilla forces and, in 123 Ce, began launching surprise attacks against the Romans. From that point on, life only got worse for the Jews. Hadrian brought an extra army legion, the "Sixth Ferrata," into Judea to deal with the terrorism. Hadrian hated "foreign" religions and forbade the Jews to perform circumcisions. He appointed Tinneius Rufus governor of Judea. Rufus was a harsh ruler who took advantage of Jewish women. In approximately 132 Ce, Hadrian began to establish a city in Jerusalem called Aelia Capitolina, the name being a combination of his own name and that of the Roman god Jupiter Capitolinus. He started to build a temple to Jupiter in place of the Jewish Holy Temple.

Shira Schoenberg also wrote the following:

> As long as Hadrian remained near Judea, the Jews stayed relatively quiet. When he left in 132, the Jews began their rebellion on a large scale. They seized towns and fortified them with walls and subterranean passages. Under the strong leadership of Shimon Bar-Kokhba, the Jews captured approximately 50 strongholds in Judea and 985 undefended towns and villages, including Jerusalem. Jews from other countries, and even some gentiles, volunteered to join their crusade...Hadrian dispatched General Publus Marcellus, governor of Syria, to help Rufus, but the Jews defeated both Roman leaders. The Jews then invaded the coastal region and the Romans began sea battles against them.

This is the Bar-Kokhba Revolt, which occurred during the years of AD 132–135. But this revolt, just like the one in AD 70, ended tragically for the Jews.

Under the leadership of General Julius Severus, Hadrian sent a legion of twelve armies from Britain, Egypt, Syria, and other areas of Judea. When General Severus reached Judea, he besieged Jewish fortresses and held back food until the Jews grew weak. Then, he waged all-out war against the Jews. The Romans destroyed every stronghold and town that belonged to the Jews. And at the final battle at Bethar, the Romans killed every single Jew. There were a few small battles that occurred in the Judean Desert Caves, but the revolt was over. Over half a million Jews were killed during this revolt. In the years following the revolt, Hadrian discriminated against all Christians, but the worst persecution was experienced by the religious Jews. The Israelites were not able to observe or practice any of their religious ordinances. The emperor also changed the name of the country Judea to Syria Palestina. And the Jews suffered persecution until the end of Hadrian's reign in AD 138.

While all of this was happening, the church was spreading farther east on the continent of Asia. The gospel of Christ was preached in ancient China, and the church was being established in that country. The ekklesia continued to increase in number and spread throughout the Roman Empire. For instance, the Celtic peregrine (missionaries) evangelized Western Europe with the apostle's doctrine. Many of the saints had their own copies of the New Testament, which was written on a certain type of paper called papyrus.

Papyrus is made from the stem of a reed or the skin of an animal treated to make leather, parchment, or vellum. During the first century, educated scribes copied the New Testament Scriptures after they were written by the apostles and disciples of Christ. These scribes were saints of God who fellowshipped with the apostles and the elect. The New Testament continued to be copied by hand during the post-apostolic age and afterward. Also, the Jewish scribes continued to copy by hand the canonized version of the Old Testament, which was canonized by the Jews at Jamnia around AD 85–90. The Jews were also printing handwritten copies of the Old Testament at Qumran, and the saints obtained copies from them. The saints had copies of the Septuagint and the Hebrew Tanakh during this time. In addition, the church was spreading all over North Africa and further south on the continent. This is how the Lord Jesus added souls to His church during the first half of the second century.

Now before I move on with the story of God's ekklesia and how it spread in the second half of the second century, I must talk about and cover an intense subject: the origins of the doctrine of the Trinity. You must realize that the Christians who were living in the Roman Empire were surrounded by people who either worshipped the gods of Rome (Greek Mythology) or were Greek philosophers. One of these people was a man named Justin. He was a gentile who was born in ancient Palestine around AD 100. He and other men such as Aristides, Athenagoras, and Theophilus of Antioch were the Greek apologists who arose during and after the post-apostolic age. Before he came in contact with Judeo-Christianity, Justin was a well-educated philosopher who was heavily influenced by the philosophies of the Hellenistic world. He trusted in the Greek philosophies in order to obtain the true knowledge of God. But after much searching and studying, Justin came to the conclusion that true knowledge was not to be found in the Greek philosophies. So around AD 130, the following event occurred in Ephesus:

> While giving himself over to his meditations by the seaside, an old man met him and began a conversation with him. The old man was a Christian. Justin argued vehemently with the old man in the defense of his pet philosophy and received very little argument in return. But finally the old man curtly cut him off: "You are a mere dealer in words, but no lover of action and truth; your aim is not to be a practiser of good, but a clever disputant, a cunning sophist." And when finally Justin put the question to the old man: "Where then is truth?" The old man replied, "Search the Scriptures and

pray that the gates of light may be opened to you, for none can perceive and comprehend these things except God and His Christ grant them understanding."

Now let me break it down to you what happened while Justin was in Asia Minor. After the old man told him about the things that are in the Tanakh and Jesus, Justin took his advice and obtained copies of the Old Testament. We know for sure that he had the five books of Moses, the Psalms, Isaiah, and some of the other books written by the prophets.

Justin searched the Scriptures and became impressed with the stability and truth of the teachings within them. He did this on his own. Then Justin decided to do his own investigation on God's ekklesia. He wanted to observe their behavior and see what the church was all about. But he wasn't able to attend any church services because the saints were being persecuted and then martyred at that time. So the only Christians that Justin saw were people who were about to die because of their faith in Jesus. He observed how the saints conducted themselves in the face of their persecutors. And based on what Justin saw, he was highly moved by the moral character and courage of the saints in the face of death. In other words, Justin thought that the saints had the right stuff. So after he had seen enough, Justin decided in his mind that he is now a Christian. I hope that you paid close attention to what has just happened.

After Justin's false conversion to Christianity, he devoted himself to vindicating the Christian religion by spreading it to the people of the Roman world. For example, the *Encyclopedia Britannica* states the following:

> After his conversion he retained his philosopher's cloak (Euseb., *Hist, Eccl.* iv II. 8), the distinctive badge of the wandering professional teacher of philosophy, and went about from place to place discussing the truths of Christianity in

the hope of bringing educated Pagans, as he himself had been brought, through philosophy to Christ.

Justin thought that he was doing the right thing. He truly believed that he was a saint. While he was doing all of this, Justin managed to obtain copies of the gospels of Matthew, Mark, and Luke. He read these books all by himself. The fact that he did this was bad because he used his knowledge of the Greek philosophies to try to understand the three gospels as well as the Old Testament. This is what caused him to develop his own interpretations of the Scriptures.

Now during the reign of Emperor Antoninus Pius (AD 138–161), Justin went to Rome, Italy. At that time, Rome had a huge population of saints. But in his mind, Justin was convinced that he already had the truth. So he started his own school of theology. He gave lectures in a classroom of his own to many people who were willing to listen to him. Also, he tried to defend his pseudo- Christian beliefs against the Gnostics of his day. It is here in Rome where Justin wrote his apologies, which were addressed to the emperor, his sons, the Roman senate, and all the Roman people. Nobody knows for sure, but it is believed that Justin wrote his first and second apologies around AD 150. In his *First Apology*, Justin wrote the following:

> For, in the name of God, the Father and Lord of the universe, and of our Saviour Jesus Christ, and of the Holy Spirit, they then receive the washing with water.

Justin continues on the subject of baptism by writing the following:

> In order that we may not remain the children of necessity and of ignorance, but may become the children of choice and knowledge, and may obtain in the water the remission of sins formerly committed, there is pronounced over him who chooses to be born again, and has repented of his sins, the name of God the Father and Lord of the universe; he

> who leads to the layer the person that is to be washed calling him by this name alone. For no one can utter the name of the ineffable God; and if any one dare to say that there is a name, he raves with a hopeless madness. And this washing is called illumination, because they who learn these things are illuminated in their understandings. And in the name of Jesus Christ, who was crucified under Pontius Pilate, and in the name of the Holy Ghost, who through the prophets foretold all things about Jesus, he who is illuminated is washed.

For the first time in world history, the Catholic formula of baptism is explicitly described on paper. And each person who chose to be baptized into the Catholic formula was immersed three times for each person of the Trinity.

No one during the first century was baptized in the name of the Father, Son, and Holy Spirit; you only read of people being baptized in the name of Jesus. This happened because Justin obtained copies of the Scriptures and tried to understand them on his own. There were others who were also doing this during Justin's time. It would have been better for him to receive the Holy Ghost and then be taught by the saints who God is. This is the perfect example of syncretism, which is an attempt to unite or reconcile opposite tenets or practices of two different philosophies or religions. Justin was trying to harmonize the Greek philosophies with Christianity, which are two complete opposites. He never abandoned his knowledge of the Greek philosophies.

Now all of us know that the Roman Catholic Church today has a list of popes that goes all the way back to the apostle Peter. He is the one who gave us the holy command on the day that the church started. But to this day, they have disobeyed Peter and the other apostles. And by disobeying them, the Catholics have disobeyed Yeshua. In fact, the first seven popes (according to the Catholic Church) were not popes at all. They were righteous preachers who were immersed into the name of Jesus and filled with the Holy Ghost. And if you do your research on these men, you will find no evidence of them ever teaching or believing in the doctrine of the Trinity.

The only man who was listed as a second-century pope who might have been the earliest key figure in developing and spreading this doctrine was Telesphorus. According to the Catholics, he is the one who instituted the tradition of Christmas Midnight Masses, the celebration of Easter on Sundays, the keeping of a seven-week Lent before Easter, and the singing of the Gloria during his pontificate. But some historians doubt that such attributions are accurate. So it not only could've been someone else who started these traditions, Telesphorus may have been a member of God's messianic community. But why would the Catholic Church identify him as the man who started these traditions without historical proof? The same reasons why they claimed Peter, Linus, and Anacletus as popes: the Catholic Church was interested in bolstering the papacy's claims to ancient supremacy. In other words, they were trying to make it seem like they're the true church of the first century. But we do know this: according to Irenaeus, Telesphorus and his followers, during the AD 130s, did choose to celebrate Easter only on Sunday. At that time, God's ekklesia throughout the known world commemorated the death of Yeshua on the fourteenth day of the Jewish month of Nisan regardless of the day of the week that it fell on. The Messiah Jesus died on this day during the first century. But regardless of this fact, Telesphorus continued to fellowship with the churches that celebrated Passover.

Hyginus was in Rome during the reign of Antoninus Pius, but very little is known about him. But we do know for sure that Pius I was in Rome along with Justin during the AD 140s. Justin was teaching people the fundamentals of his pseudo-Christian doctrine, and he had many followers. Now I must say this because it's the truth: Pius I, and all of the men before him, were not popes at all. There was no single ruling bishop in Rome at that time. This is true in regards to both God's ekklesia in

Rome and the Roman Church. There were only small groups of people who had pastors or bishops over them within the Catholic community. Also, the term *pope*, which comes from the Latin word for *father*, wasn't even used by the early Roman bishops. They were just men who were leaders of their own congregations. Now Pius I had his chance to be saved the Bible way. But he, like Justin, tried to learn what the Scriptures teach about God and salvation on his own. As a result, he came up with an interpretation of Scripture that was similar to Justin's.

Now I cannot say that Pius I was a pupil of Justin, but they definitely worked together in order to spread their version of the gospel of Jesus Christ. A scholar named Frederick A. Norwood wrote the following:

> Apologists could defend the faith against external threats, but who would protect it from dangers within? Who could say what was truth and what was falsehood? In response to these many challenges, both without and within, defenses were developed which offered both assurance against heresy and a basis for new growth. These included an authoritative leadership, a formal canon of scripture, and a systematic theology. The result was the institution of the ancient catholic, i.e. universal church.

And since the Catholics were convinced that they were of the truth, every saint of God who came to them saying and teaching the truth about Yeshua and salvation was labeled a heretic. Pius I was perhaps the first pre-pope, and the Roman Church's system of Catholicism was operating in Rome by AD 140. So Justin and the other apologists invented the theology of the Roman Catholic Church.

The word *catholic* comes from the Greek word *katholikos*, which means complete, whole, and universal. This Greek word also means "according to the whole." Most of the saints spoke Greek in the Roman Empire, and Ignatius used this word to describe the church of God in his letter to the Smyrnaeans. There is nothing wrong with the Greek word for *catholic*, for it describes who we are as God's elect. We are complete because Yeshua made us complete in Him, and we're whole because Yeshua has made us whole. Also, the church is universal only because God wants to save all Jews, gentiles, and peoples of mixed blood. This word was used sporadically within the ekklesia. And when the Greek apologists heard this word being used by the saints, they also used it to describe themselves because they thought that the theology that they were spreading was similar to the saint's theology. But at this time, they believed that there was a God the Father and a Son of God. The ancient Catholics were not exactly sure what the Holy Spirit was.

God's messianic community believes that there is one God who is a Spirit. That Spirit is holy by nature, so He is called the Holy Spirit. That same Spirit created everything in the beginning, so that Spirit is God the Father. And when the time had come for Him to fulfill His word, God the Father visibly revealed Himself in a Man so that all of us can see God for who He is through the face of Jesus the Messiah. God created Him to be a perfect and sinless man with His own perfect and sinless masculine human nature. And God fused Himself together with His spirit. In other words, the true God put Himself inside the physical body of Jesus Christ and fused Himself together with His perfect and sinless human nature. He did this without ceasing to be God. This is why Yeshua told the Jews, "I and My Father are One." Jesus the Messiah is God manifest in the flesh. So during the thirties and forties of the second century, there were two different churches operating on earth: God's original and primitive ekklesia and the Roman Catholic Church. God's true church is at least one hundred years older than the Catholic Church.

Throughout his life in Rome, Justin continued to write letters to the Catholic Church. He even wrote about a long conversation he had with a Jewish man named Trypho. Justin wrote, "For the prophetical gifts remain with us, even to the present time." He also wrote, "Now, it is possible to see amongst us women and men who possess gifts of the Spirit of God." Justin's long dialogue with Trypho gives us some evidence that the ancient Roman Catholic Church was indeed Pentecostal. After all, the Catholic Church in Rome was severely outnumbered and surrounded by saints who spoke in other tongues and had the various gifts of the Spirit. The Catholics wanted to be like the ekklesia. And since God wants to save everybody, He filled many of them with the Holy Ghost! Also, God was able to lead some of the Catholics to the knowledge of the truth so that they would be baptized in the name of Jesus Christ. The people who were baptized again fellowshipped with God's elect. But most of them were stubborn against God. Not only did they refuse to be baptized again, they remained in the Catholic system.

Justin taught his doctrine of the Logos. Bro. David K. Bernard wrote the following:

> This trend toward trinitarianism began by making the Logos (the Word of John 1) a separate person. Following a thought in Greek philosophy, particularly in the teachings of Philo, some of the Greek apologists began to view the Logos as a separate person from the Father...To them the Father alone was the real God and the Logos was a created divine being of second rank. Eventually, the Logos became equated with the Son.

Now God's ekklesia believes that the Logos is the mind of God. And in God's mind, He had a plan to redeem mankind before the creation of everything. And this plan came to fruition when God revealed Himself in the flesh and died on the cross. This is what the New Testament teaches the church, but Justin refused to embrace this doctrine due to his carnal mind. The Catholic Church continued to use the New Testament to teach their heretical doctrine, and it began to spread throughout the Roman Empire.

As for the other apologists, little is known about them. But we do know this: Theophilus of Antioch, who was deeply influenced by Stoicism, allegedly became a Christian through his personal study of the Scriptures. Let me repeat that: *his personal study of the Scriptures*! So Theophilus became a Christian in his own mind by studying the Holy Scriptures on his own. Also, he decided to spread his understanding of Christianity by harmonizing Greek philosophy and Stoicism with Christianity. And because he was knowledgeable of the Greek philosophies, Theophilus, like Justin, naturally came up with the same interpretations of Scripture. And throughout his life, he wrote a few books, including his Catholic commentary on the book of Genesis.

Aristides, another Greek philosopher, came in contact with Christianity without converting to it. For instance, he wrote the following in his apology that was addressed to Emperor Antoninus Pius:

> But the Christians, O King, while they went about and made search, have found the truth; and as we learned from their writings, they have come nearer to truth and genuine knowledge than the rest of the nations.

Many scholars believe that this apology was addressed to Hadrian, but the most complete version of this apology says that it was Hadrian's successor. But anyway, Aristides is telling the emperor that he obtained copies of the Bible and read the Scriptures on his own. Apparently, he wasn't alone when he did this. Aristides wanted to be like the saints, but he wouldn't abandon his knowledge of the Greek philosophies.

All the apologists were carnal, and they tried to understand the dual nature of the Messiah Jesus without His help. And this lack of spiritual knowledge is the foundation of the doctrine of the Trinity.

Lastly, a man named Tatian came on the theological scene during the time of Justin. He was born in ancient Assyria, and in his adult years, he traveled to Rome, Italy. While in Rome, Tatian met Justin and became his disciple during the AD 150s. He received his theological training from Justin. As a result, he would become another apologist defending Catholicism against the Gnostics.

Now during the AD 150s, Polycarp was still serving as the bishop of the ekklesia in ancient Smyrna. Despite the rise of the Catholic Church, Polycarp remained true to the faith. Little is known about his life and ministry, but we do know that Polycarp wrote his own letter to the saints at Philippi. We also know that Anicetus (AD 154–167) succeeded Pius I in AD 154 and became the bishop of the Roman Church during Polycarp's time. After this happened, Polycarp went to Rome to meet Anicetus to discuss the date for the celebration of Pascha. The churches in Asia Minor were still commemorating the death of Jesus Christ on the exact date of the Jewish Passover, regardless of the day of the week. But the Catholic churches, along with the followers of Anicetus, were using a specific Sunday each year. They couldn't come to an agreement, so both decided to leave their traditions as they were. But despite their disagreements, they celebrated communion with one another. Even though he did this, there is no historical proof that Polycarp conformed to the teachings of Catholicism. He went back to Smyrna and resumed his apostolic ministry.

Toward the end of his life, Polycarp was captured and sentenced to death because he refused to renounce Jesus and proclaim that Caesar is Lord. He was taken to a stadium in Smyrna, bound, and surrounded with wood and fuel in order to be burned alive. When they lit the fire, something miraculous happened: the fire didn't consume him and he wasn't harmed at all. As a result of this, the executioner plunged a dagger into Polycarp and killed him instantly. So much blood gushed out of him that it quenched the fire that was supposed to kill him. After he died, Polycarp's body was burned. But prior to his death, Polycarp mentioned to his executioners that he has served the Lord for eighty-six years. Polycarp was not born and raised in the faith, but he did get saved at an early age. So it is more than likely that he died during the AD 160s. But regardless of the date of his death, we do know that Polycarp was martyred as a saint of God.

During the year AD 161, one of the most renowned men in the history of the Roman Empire ascended to the throne: Marcus Aurelius. He was a well-educated man and a philosopher. During his reign, most of the citizens of the empire considered Marcus to be a just, kind, and amiable emperor. He also displayed his leadership during the Marcomannic and Quadi Wars. But Emperor Aurelius, just like Trajan and Hadrian before him, had a big problem with Christianity. In fact, Marcus Aurelius developed his empire with the strongest system of philosophy which made anti-Christian literature flourish for the first time. Samson Hutagalung wrote the following:

> Because of the widespread of this literature to the whole empire, the hatred of the public increased toward Christianity. As a result when the emperor decreed persecution against Christianity, those who were loyal to the emperor actually joined to persecute Christians.

Hutagalung also wrote the following:

> The emperor Marcus Aurelius (161–180) decreed that the property of Christians should be given to their accusers. It is not difficult to see what would be the effect to this decree. Everywhere there were people who were eager to have the property of the Christians.

> These came forward with accusations. Persecution became well nigh universal. Christians everywhere were sought out, brought to trial, and often executed with the greatest cruelty, while their property was taken from them and given to their accusers.

It doesn't take a great imagination to know how dark a period this was for God's ekklesia. The saints were fed to wild beasts, beheaded, and in some cases tortured to death. God's elect died in other various ways as well. But despite this horrible persecution, the saints of God were still able to win souls for Christ throughout the empire. This is the result of God's power and His ability to draw men unto Himself. And because of God's power in His saints, the ekklesia maintained their faith in Jesus till the very end of their lives. This persecution did not end until the year that Aurelius died.

Even the Catholics, like the elect, suffered persecution and martyrdom during Aurelius's reigns. This happened to them because the world did not know the difference between them and God's ekklesia. For example: During the year AD 165, Justin and six of his companions were captured and brought to Rusticus the Perfect. According to the *Catholic Encyclopedia*, the following event occurred:

> The Prefect Rusticus says: Approach and sacrifice, all of you, to the gods. Justin says: No one in his right mind gives up piety for impiety. The Prefect Rusticus says: If you do not obey, you will be tortured without mercy. Justin replies: That is our desire, to be tortured for Our Lord, Jesus Christ, and so to be saved, for that will give us salvation and firm confidence at the more terrible universal tribunal of Our Lord and Saviour. And all the martyrs said: Do as you wish; for we are Christians, and we do not sacrifice to idols.

After they said this to him, Rusticus sentenced all of them to death. So Justin and his companions were scourged and then beheaded.

Now I must say this before I move on: Justin had his chance to be saved when the old man tried to witness to him in Ephesus. But he was stubborn against him and the truth. At the same time, Justin was curious about the Scriptures, so he sought the truth that is in them. But he did this without God's help. As a result of his actions, Justin invented a formula of baptism that is completely foreign to the New Testament. And throughout his ministry, Justin refused to be corrected about the truth of biblical salvation. He was never able to come to the knowledge of the truth about who God is. So Justin and his companions fell asleep that day with the Catholics who died before him. And to add insult to injury, the *Encyclopedia Britannica* states the following:

> There are not many traces of any particular literary influence of his writings upon the Christian Church, and this need not surprise us. The Church as a whole took but little interest in apologetics and polemics, nay, had at times even an instinctive feeling that in these controversies that which she held holy might easily suffer loss. Thus Justin's writings were not much read, and at the present time both the *Apology* and the *Dialogue* are preserved in but a single MS. (cod. Paris, 450, AD 1364)

In other words, Justin's writings weren't popular in the second century, even amongst Catholics. Justin has no one to blame but himself. Other Catholics died as well throughout Aurelius's reign. And after Justin's death, Catholicism continued to be practiced in the Roman Church.

While Justin lived, Tatian remained faithful to the Catholic Church. But later on in his life, Tatian renounced his faith in Catholicism and left the Roman Church. Howbeit that he was a Catholic apologist who defended Catholicism against Gnosticism. But for whatever reason he apostatized, became a Gnostic of the Encratite sect, and returned to the Orient in AD 172. Prior to doing this, Tatian wrote about the Catholic formula of baptism in his work called the *Diatessaron*. He wrote the following:

> Go now into all the world, and preach my gospel in all the creation; and teach all the peoples, and baptize them in the name of the Father and the Son and the Holy Spirit; and teach them to keep all whatsoever I commanded you: and lo, I am with you all the days, unto the end of the world. For whosoever believeth and is baptized shall be saved; but whosoever believeth not shall be rejected.

Now it is obvious that Tatian is quoting Matthew 28:19 and Mark 16:16. The problem is not that he's quoting the Scriptures, but it is the fact that he and his follow Catholics were repeating the instructions of the Lord rather than following them. It is not known what happened to Tatian after he became a Gnostic. But I do know this: If Tatian never embraced the gospel of Christ according to the Scriptures, then he entered into eternity without *Yeshua*.

Athenagoras of Athens is another man who was a philosopher who converted to Catholicism. After his conversion, he worked as an apologist during the second half of the second century. He wrote an apology that was addressed to Marcus Aurelius and his son Commodus in AD 177. Athenagoras also wrote his "Treatise on the Resurrection." Other than his two writings, very little is known about Athenagoras's life. But it is safe to say that he remained faithful to the Roman Church. He fell asleep with his fellow Catholics around AD 190. And prior to his death, Theophilus of Antioch fell asleep between AD 183–185.

During the last few years of Aurelius's reign, Irenaeus (AD 115–200?) was serving as the bishop of his own church in ancient Lugdunum (modern -day Lyons, France). Not much is known about his life. But we do know this: Irenaeus met Polycarp while he was a child in Smyrna. He would grow up in the faith and become Polycarp's disciple. So Irenaeus was baptized in the name of Jesus Christ, and God filled him with the *Ruach Ha-Kodesh* (Aramaic for Holy Spirit). It is possible that he was born and raised in the faith, but nobody knows for sure. While he was in Asia Minor, Irenaeus remained in the ekklesia of Jesus. But prior to Justin's death, Irenaeus went to Rome and joined the school of Justin. Why he went to Rome is not certain, but he became a follower of Justin because the things of God that he learned since childhood did not remain in his heart. So Irenaeus left the faith and joined the Catholic Church.

In AD 180, Irenaeus wrote a five- volume series of books that is titled *Adversus Haereses* (Latin for Against Heresies). Irenaeus wrote these books for the sole purpose of refuting the Gnostics of his day. He targeted the Valentinian Gnostics who not only had a distorted view of Christ, they believed that there are three classes of human beings. According these Gnostics, the first class of people are material beings who cannot obtain salvation, the second class of people are psychics who are part of the church, and the third class of people are spiritual beings who cannot decay or be harmed by material actions.

There were other sects of Gnosticism and heretics that existed during the second century. For example: The Docetists believed that Jesus was only a spirit being. The Cerinthians believed that there was a man named Jesus and a divine being called the Christ. Also, they believed that the divine Christ temporarily dwelt in Jesus beginning at His baptism but withdrew from the man Jesus just before His death. These are doctrines of Gnosticism, which means salvation through secret knowledge. The Holy Bible teaches salvation through Jesus the Messiah. In addition, there were other Gnostic teachings about Jesus as well. There were the Adoptionists who believed that Jesus wasn't completely human, and the Marcionists who believed that the Old Testament God was evil while the New Testament God was good. None of these heretics were a threat to God's original and primitive ekklesia. Only the new saints who just got saved were susceptible to their doctrines. As long as they remained in the church, they learned the truth that is in the apostle's doctrine. But these heretical groups were a threat to the Catholic Church because the Catholics were small in number, and the development of the doctrine of the Trinity was still in its infancy. This doctrine is built on a foundation of sand, so it was susceptible to the teachings of the Gnostics.

In addition to being a Catholic, Irenaeus taught doctrines that are completely foreign to the Holy Bible. For example, Irenaeus believed that humanity was created immature, and God intended His creatures to take a long time to grow into His likeness. This led him to believe that Adam and Eve were created as children. So according to Irenaeus, their Fall was thus not a full-blown rebellion but a childish spat, a desire to grow up before their time and have everything now. Not even the Catholics of today, nor of the second century, believe this to be true. In addition to this false teaching, Irenaeus believed that Jesus lived to be an old man and that His public ministry lasted at least ten years. And how do I know this?

This information is in his five-volume work titled *Against Heresies*. Now what Bible did he get all of this from? Who taught him this nonsense? The answer: Irenaeus came up with this foolishness all by himself. He is another example of what happens when you leave the truth, embrace doctrines that are foreign to the Holy Bible, and try to understand the Scriptures by using your own human intellect.

The irony in all of this is that the same man who wrote *Against Heresies* became a heretic himself. Also, Irenaeus wrote a book that is titled *Demonstration of the Apostolic Preaching*. In his book, Irenaeus wrote the following:

> We have received baptism…for the remission of sins in the name of God the Father, and in the name of Jesus Christ the Son of God, who was incarnate and died and rose again, and in the Holy Spirit of God.

History records that Irenaeus was not a man who believed in the Trinity. In fact, his writings show proof that he did retain some of the things that he learned from Polycarp and the saints. But by AD 190, he abandoned water baptism in the name of Jesus Christ.

Now no one knows for sure what happened to Irenaeus during the last decade of his life. He either died toward the end of the second century or the beginning of the third. I just hope that he returned to God and renounced the things that he learned from Justin and the other Roman Catholics. If he did this, then he is currently in heaven with the rest of the saints of God. But if he remained a Catholic, then he fell asleep with the rest of the Catholic Fathers of the second century.

In summary, the Roman Catholic Church had its own theology concerning the Godhead. But it wasn't completely established during the second century. For example, Justin wrote the following in his apology:

> Our teacher of these things is Jesus Christ, who also was born for this purpose, and was crucified under Pontius Pilate, procurator of Judaea, in the times of Tiberius Caesar; and that we reasonably worship Him, having learned that He is the Son of the true God Himself, and holding Him in the second place, and the prophetic Spirit in the third, we will prove. For they proclaim our madness to consist in this, that we give to a crucified man a place second to the unchangeable and eternal God, the Creator of all; for they do not discern the mystery that is herein, to which, as we make it plain to you, we pray you to give heed.

It's obvious that Justin believes that God the Father is first, the Son of God is second, and the Holy Spirit is third. Also, he doesn't describe them as coequal. In fact, Justin implies a rank within the Godhead. This means that God the Father, in Justin's mind, is the most important being in the Godhead.

Justin viewed the Logos as a created being that is divine. He eventually equated the Logos with the Son of God. Catholic scholar R. L. Richard wrote the following:

> For Justin, the Godhead was very clearly a *Triad*, though it was Theophilus (*Ad Autol.* 2.15) who first introduced this expression. For Justin, the Word is no less than *something numerically other* (*Dial.* 128) in relation to the Father, and also, though more loosely affirmed (e.g., 1 *Apol.* 60–63), to the Spirit. In the very same passages, however, neither Word nor Spirit, the former more explicitly, are to be separated

from the Father, from the being of the Godhead, since both Word and Spirit are God.

Mr. Richard also wrote the following:

> Justin pictures the preexistent Word as the Father's rational consciousness (1 *Apol.* 46; 2 *Apol.* 13), as emerging, therefore, from the interiority of the Godhead while nevertheless remaining inseparable from the Godhead. Tatian employs much of the same explanatory machinery (*Orat.* 5), likewise Theophilus (*Ad Autol.* 2.10; 2.22). So also does Athenagoras (*Legat.* 10), who extends the imagery to the third member and speaks of the Spirit here as God's effluence.

Not only was the Logos doctrine believed on in the Catholic Church, the majority of Catholics viewed Jesus Christ as being subordinate to the Father. The Catholic apologists were successful in developing their systematic theology. But they couldn't clearly define their theology as to how the Father, the Son, and the Holy Spirit are one God. So for the next two centuries, the doctrine of the Trinity will continue to evolve until a solution was finalized.

Before I move on I must make this point to you, dear reader. I'm not judging any of these men of the past. In fact, I'm not trying to judge anyone today. I'm just bringing out the facts more clearly. If you believe that you're a Christian no matter what, fine. Today, there are over forty thousand Christian denominations worldwide, and all of them say that they are Christians. And if you tell me that you're a Christian, I will not try to convince you otherwise. But the facts are the facts! And the reality is this: not all Christians are saints, but all *saints* are Christians (Matt. 7:21–23). And if you take heed to what this book has to say, then you can become a saint as well. I say this because I love you and Jesus loves you more than I do.

After Polycarp's death, there were still thousands of pastors/preachers who were willing to hold up the blood-stained banner, which is the apostle's doctrine. But only several of them are recorded in world history. So I will only talk about these holy men of God. Noetus of Smyrna was a preacher of righteous who lived during the second and third centuries. He was Praxeas's teacher in Asia Minor. After he had learned enough from his teacher, Praxeas traveled to Rome and established his own church there. We know for sure that he was preaching the apostle's doctrine in Rome about AD 190. I'll talk about him and Noetus some more in the next chapter. It is also very possible that the following men were apostolic preachers in Asia Minor: Thraseas, Sagaris, Papirius, Melito, and Polycrates.

Now I, unlike the Catholics, am not trying to claim any of these men as members of the ancient apostolic church. If any of them were baptized in the name of Jesus and filled with the Holy Ghost, then they were members of God's messianic community. But if they were Catholic, then they were members of the Roman Church. In fact, I don't have to claim any man or woman from the first and second centuries in order for me to prove to you that the original and primitive church taught the apostle's doctrine. The book of Acts does that for me. All you have to do is read the Acts of the Apostles. So I'm not claiming anyone in this book. But all of these men have two things in common: They oversaw their own churches in Asia Minor, and they commemorated the death of Christ on the fourteenth day of the Jewish month of Nisan. The celebration of Easter only on Sundays came from the Roman Catholic Church. And the Catholics are Trinitarians.

Now I am not trying to start a debate on how to celebrate Passover. Once again, I'm just bringing out the facts about the Catholics and the churches in Asia Minor. (I'm pretty sure that you don't worship the goddess of the dawn.) And since the Catholic Church was strict on celebrating Easter only on Sundays, history records that no Catholics celebrated Easter on no other day of the week during the second century. James F. Kenney wrote the following:

> It is probable that the primitive Christians kept the Pasch on the 14th of Nisan as determined by the Jewish authorities, and regarded it as the anniversary of the crucifixion. But they also observed the first of every seven days, the Jewish week, as a holy day in commemoration of the resurrection… Accordingly the majority of Christians (Roman Catholics) celebrated the Pasch not on the 14th of Nisan but on the Sunday which it fell on, or first after, that date. The churches of the Roman province of Asia, however, followed the older custom, keeping the Pasch on the 14th of Nisan, whatever the day of the week.

You can try to speculate that perhaps a very small number of Catholics celebrated the Pasch only on Passover, but there's no historical proof of this. In addition to commemorating the death of Jesus only on Passover, some of these five preachers from Asia Minor wrote books while others wrote letters to the churches, the emperor of Rome, and the Catholics. For instance, Melito wrote an apology that was addressed to Marcus Aurelius. But most of these preacher's works were destroyed. The ones that survived have no Trinitarian concepts or theology in it whatsoever. Even the various Catholic encyclopedias of today know this to be true. This is especially true of Polycrates. He wrote a letter to Victor I (AD 189–199) while he was the bishop in Rome. In his letter, Polycrates stated that he rejects Victor's authority as the bishop of the Roman Church. Also, he stated that he will continue to observe the Pasch on the day of the Jewish Passover regardless of the day of the week. If these men were not members of God's ekklesia, history gives us no proof that they were Catholic in their theology. All of these men died during the second century.

As for the rest of the church, God's original and primitive ekklesia continued to spread and increase in number throughout the known world. This is partially due to the fact that the churches enjoyed a time of peace after Aurelius's death. *Elohim* (God in Hebrew) was drawing men and women unto Himself. So the ekklesia increased in number in ancient England, Gaul, and Spain. People were being baptized into the name of Yeshua the Messiah, and the Holy Ghost was falling like rain on these people. Hundreds were getting saved in some areas while thousands were being added to the church in other areas of the empire. The ekklesia even spread to the Goths and other Germanic tribes beyond the boundaries of the Roman Empire.

During the seventies of this century, the Ethiopian ekklesia challenged the Catholics who came to them. This happened because the Catholics came to one of their churches talking about their concept of the Godhead. Once again, the Roman Catholics thought that their theology was identical to the doctrine of Christ. But after meeting the Ethiopian apostolics, the Catholics saw the differences between them and God's ekklesia. Hence, they were rejected. The Lord Jesus continued to add souls to His church on the continent of Africa. The seventies is also the period of time when the early ideas about purgatory, catechism, and confirmation seeped into Catholicism; these things were adopted from the Orphic cult.

The ekklesia continued to increase in number in the city of Rome, and they outnumbered the Roman Catholics. Perhaps this is why they tried to persecute the churches in Africa and Europe. But due to their small size, their persecution against God's ekklesia was at best minor. Also, the gospel of Christ continued to be preached on the continent of Asia. As a result, the tongue-talkers of God increased in number, especially in the Parthian Empire, Bactria, Media, and Persia. God's church also increased in number in ancient Arabia, India, and China. Throughout the known world, the churches of Yeshua were living in a time of peace toward the end of the second century. So the saints marched triumphantly into the third century, still anticipating the coming of the Son of God.

THE THIRD CENTURY

The first two years of the third century was a peaceful time for the messianic community in the Roman Empire. The *Ruach Kodesh* (Hebrew for Holy Spirit) was with His churches, and He was drawing men and women unto Himself. As a result, many souls were added to the ekklesia. But things changed during the year AD 202. This is when Emperor Septimius Severus (AD 193–211) enacted a rigid law that forbade all Roman citizens to join Christianity and Judaism. As a result of this law, many Catholics, Jews, and saints of God were brutally killed in the empire. For example, a saint named Basilides, a preacher of righteousness, was martyred in AD 204. (He is not to be confused with other men who share the same name in the third century.) Also, Clement of Alexandria wrote, "Many martyrs are daily burned, confined or beheaded, before our eyes." This was a terrible time in the Roman Empire. But despite all the things that the ekklesia suffered, God still added souls to His church and many saints survived this persecution. Sometimes, God allows bad things to happen to His people so that He can display His power and preeminence over all things. Yeshua has to do this so that we can trust and depend on Him. It may be painful, but the trials of the saints always work out for our good. So God's elect, with the help of Jesus, endured great persecution till the end of Severus's reign.

The first thirty-plus years of the third century was a very interesting period of time for the Catholic Church. I say this because of the first two bishops of the Roman Church and the things that happened during this period. The first bishop was a man named Zephyrinus (AD 199–217). Despite the fact that he served as bishop for almost twenty years, little is known about him. But we do know this: the members of the Catholic Church were unhappy with him being the bishop of Rome.

Hippolytus (AD 170?–236) was the main reason for this. He was an avowed adherent of the Trinitarian doctrine of the Logos. For instance, he taught that the Logos became man in Christ, differs in every thing from God, and that He is the mediary between God and the world of creatures, particularly man. Zephyrinus, unlike the Catholics, clung firmly to the doctrine that he claimed was handed down from the apostles. Johann Kirsch wrote the following:

> Pope Zephyrinus did not interpose authoritatively in the dispute between the two schools. The heresy of the Modalists was not at first clearly evident, and the doctrine of Hippolytus offered many difficulties as regards the tradition of the Church. Zephyrinus said simply that he acknowledged only one God, and this was the Lord Jesus Christ, but it was the Son, not the Father, Who had died.

Hippolytus had no problems with Zephyrinus's statement (even though it expressed God being one). He just wanted Zephyrinus to approve a Trinitarian doctrine which emphasizes the Person of Christ being completely different from the Father. Also, he wanted the bishop to condemn the prevalent doctrine of the ekklesia, which the Catholics called Modalism or Monarchianism. Zephyrinus refused to do so. As a result, Hippolytus charged Zephyrinus with laxity in enforcing discipline and failure to assert his authority sufficiently in repressing the Monarchian doctrine. And according to Hippolytus, the apostolic doctrine of Christ was heresy.

As time went on, Hippolytus and others like him became angrier at the bishop. In fact, Hippolytus was completely against Zephyrinus and accused him of Modalism. No historian or scholar knows for sure, but Zephyrinus may have embraced Modalism. And if this is true, that would make him a member of God's messianic community. Once again, I'm not trying to rewrite history or say anything about Zephyrinus that isn't already known. I'm just bringing out the facts more clearly for everyone. Zephyrinus served as the bishop of Rome till he died in AD 217.

Sabellius, a saint and preacher of holiness, was in Rome during the time of Zephyrinus. He taught the apostle's doctrine, which was prevalent in Rome. The Catholics called the apostle's doctrine Monarchianism because it emphasizes above all the absolute unity (*monarchia*) of God. And according the Catholics, this doctrine explains the incarnation of Christ in the sense that this was another manifestation (*modus*) of God in His union with the human nature of Christ. In other words, this doctrine teaches that there is one God, and the Son of God is that same one God and a sinless man fused together. The Catholics heard the truth of God, but they refused to accept it. And since the ekklesia adheres to the apostle's doctrine, they were also called Modalists or *Patripassians* (the Father Himself suffered). The ekklesia knows that the Father did not suffer anything, but He was in His Son during His sufferings. And Sabellius's doctrine was called Sabellianism.

After Zephyrinus died, Callistus I, Zephyrinus's deacon and confidential counselor, became the bishop of the Roman Catholic Church. Prior to Zephyrinus's death, Hippolytus believed that Callistus I was responsible for Zephyrinus's refusal to approve a Trinitarian doctrine and condemn Monarchianism. So when Callistus I became the bishop of the Roman Church, Hippolytus and his followers withdrew from the Catholic Church, caused the first schism in the Catholic

Church's history, and made himself a rival bishop. So Hippolytus and his followers were the first group of people to separate themselves from the Catholic Church before it officially became the Catholic Church. (If you're a historian, then you know exactly what I mean.) They did this because of the things that Callistus I did. For example, Callistus I admitted to communion with those who had done public penance for murder, adultery, and fornication. Hippolytus was outraged because of this.

Now according to most scholars, Callistus I condemned Sabellius because of his doctrine. But these same scholars also know that Hippolytus was against Callistus I because he was too friendly to the Monarchians. So why would Callistus I condemn Sabellius but have no problems with the rest of the tongue-talking ekklesia of God? Perhaps the answer was given to us by two scholars named H. Wace and C. C. Bunsen. They have both suggested that Callistus's action was motivated more by a desire for unity in the Catholic Church rather than by conviction. Also, there is no historical evidence that Callistus I was any champion of the Trinitarian doctrine. In fact, he may have experienced the new birth. But if he didn't, then that's on him. In addition, Callistus I allowed the lower clergy to marry, and permitted noble ladies to marry low persons and slaves, which by the Roman law was forbidden. Hippolytus was against this as well. He also accused Callistus I of permitting bishops married more than once to serve, women into religious study, pre-marital sex, contraception, abortion, and marriage outside of one's own social status. But most of today's scholars believe that Hippolytus was trying to slander Callistus I. And prior to his death, Hail Marys, cuttings and self-tortures became part of the Catholic experience. Callistus I died in AD 222.

After his death, Urban I became the Bishop of Rome. But despite the change in leadership, Hippolytus and his followers remained separate from the Catholic Church. Very little is known about Urban's life. We just know that Hippolytus wasn't satisfied when Urban I was elected

Bishop of Rome. After Urban's death in AD 230, Pontian was elected Bishop of the Catholic Church. It is during this time that Hippolytus and his followers ended their schism and rejoined the Catholic Church in Rome. Like I said, this was a very interesting period of time for the Roman Catholic Church.

During the time of Bishop Zephyrinus, Hippolytus described the Trinitarian formula of baptism in one of his works. Hippolytus wrote the following:

> When the one being baptized goes down into the water, the one baptizing him shall put his hand on him and speak thus: "Do you believe in God, the Father Almighty?" And he that is being baptized shall say: "I believe." Then, having his hand imposed upon the head of the one to be baptized, he shall baptize him once. Then he shall say: "Do you believe in Christ Jesus…?" And when he says: "I believe," he is baptized again. Again shall he say: 'Do you believe in the Holy Spirit and the holy Church and the resurrection of the flesh?" The one being baptized then says: "I believe." And so he is baptized a third time.

This is how the Catholic Church baptized their new converts into their church in the third century. Each new convert was immersed three times into each person of the Trinity. The New Testament only speaks of the apostles baptizing new converts once into the name of Jesus Christ.

Now the doctrine of the Trinity continued to take on its evolution during the third century. But in order for me to cover this, I must backtrack to the second century. Since the birth of the Catholic Church, the concept of one God who has revealed Himself in three persons (Father, Son, and Holy Spirit) did not have a name to identify itself. But this changed when Quintus Septimius Florens Tertullianus (a.k.a. Tertullian) came on the scene. He was born in Carthage located in

North Africa around AD 150. All that we know about his life is in his ancient writings that have survived. So we know that Tertullian studied Greek philosophy, Plato, and the writings of the Stoics. At some point in his life, Tertullian left Carthage and traveled to Rome, Italy. While in Rome, he converted to Catholicism around AD 190. But the circumstances of his conversion are unknown. After his conversion, Tertullian stayed in Rome for a while. The *Encyclopedia Britannica* states the following:

> He bent himself with all his energy to the study of Scripture and of Christian literature. Not only was he master of the contents of the Bible: he also read carefully the works of Hermas, Justin, Tatian, Miltiades, Melito, Irenaeus, Proculus, Clement, as well as many Gnostic treatises, the writings Marcion in particular.

Now I admire his dedication to increase in knowledge, but the Holy Scriptures are complete all by themselves. Tertullian would've done much better to ask God to open up his understanding of the scriptures. From Rome, he traveled to Greece, and then he left Greece to visit the Catholic churches in Asia Minor. Once he felt that he had learned enough, Tertullian went back to Carthage and laid the foundation of Latin Catholic literature.

Throughout the rest of his life, Tertullian wrote over three dozen books and letters. In some of his writings Tertullian teaches his theology and what it takes to be saved. For example, in one of his works titled "On Baptism," Tertullian wrote the following:

> For the law of baptizing has been imposed, and the formula prescribed: "Go," He saith, "teach the nations, baptizing them into the name of the FATHER, AND OF THE SON, AND OF THE HOLY SPIRIT." The comparison with the law of that definition, "Unless a man have been reborn of

water and Spirit, he shall not enter into the kingdom of the heavens," has tied faith to the necessity of baptism.

In another work, Tertullian wrote the following:

> Hereupon WE ARE THRICE IMMERSED, making a somewhat ampler pledge than the Lord has appointed in the Gospel.

Now it's obvious that Tertullian believes that water baptism is mandatory to obtain salvation, but he is commanding his readers to repeat the instructions of the Lord Jesus rather than follow them. Doing these things does not please the Spirit of the Living God.

Tertullian continued to write about his theological beliefs. In another work that he wrote to refute the teachings of Praxeas (a member of God's ekklesia), Tertullian wrote the following:

> As if in this way also one were not All, in that All are of One, by unity (that is) of substance; while the mystery of the dispensation is still guarded, which distributes the Unity into a Trinity, placing in their order the three Persons—the Father, the Son, and the Holy Ghost: three, however, not in condition, but in degree; not in substance, but in form; not in power, but in aspect; yet of one substance, and of one condition, and of one power, inasmuch as He is one God.

For the first time in human history, the word *trinity*, which comes from the Latin word *trinitas*, is used to describe the Catholic God as being three divine persons and yet one God. The word *trinitas* is Latin for *threeness*. And last but not least, Tertullian wrote the following:

> He commands them to baptize into THE FATHER AND THE SON AND THE HOLY GHOST, not into a unipersonal God. And indeed it is not once only, but three

times, that we are immersed into the Three Persons, at each several mention of Their names.

I can go on and on about Tertullian's theological beliefs, but I won't to save time. The information that I have brought out proves one thing: Tertullian is the father of Trinitarianism. The reason why Tertullian had no problems with the Trinity is because it is impossible to understand the idea and logic of it. According to David K. Bernard, Tertullian's whole theology rested on the thought that the more impossible the object of faith is, the more certain it is. So Tertullian believed that the Trinity exists because it cannot be comprehended. His letter against the teachings of Praxeas is believed to be dated in AD 216.

Since his conversion to Catholicism, Tertullian was an active member of the Roman Church, especially in Carthage. He was an evangelist and presbyter who worked hard to fortify the Catholic Church against the Gnostics that were in Carthage during his day. But things began to change for Tertullian during the years of AD 202–203. It is during these years that he began to recognize the New Prophecy movement. This movement was started by a man named Montanus during the second century. He emphasized the gifts of the Spirit, but he also claimed to be the Paraclete (Comforter). Montanus even claimed to be the last prophet before the end of the world. For whatever reason, Tertullian was captivated by this movement. The *Encyclopedia Britannica* states the following:

> It was his desire to unite the enthusiasm of primitive Christianity with intelligent thought, the original demands of the Gospel with every letter of the Scriptures and with the practice of the Roman Church, the sayings of the Paraclete with the authority of the bishops, the law of the churches with the freedom of the inspired, the rigid discipline of the Montanist with all the utterances of the New Testament

and with the arrangements of a church seeking to set itself up within the world.

Tertullian worked hard to do these things for the next several years, but he failed. He became angry and frustrated with the Roman Church. So in the year AD 207, Tertullian left the Catholic Church, joined the New Prophecy movement and became the head of a small Montanist community in Carthage. Then he became the most powerful representative of the New Prophecy movement in the west. Tertullian never went back to the Catholic Church. And during the last decades of his life, he continued to do battle with the Catholic Church, the Gnostics, and the ekklesia of God. Tertullian fell asleep with his fellow Trinitarians in AD 222. He is viewed as a Catholic Church father even though he died as a prominent member of the New Prophecy.

Prior to Tertullian's conversion to Catholicism, the Catechetical School of Alexandria in Egypt, according to most scholars, was founded in AD 180 (others say AD 190). The first head of this school was a man named Pantaenus, and he is probably the school's founder. Little is known about him, but we do know that Pantaenus was a Stoic philosopher who converted to Catholicism. His legacy is known by the influence of the catechetical school on the development of Catholic theology, the Trinitarian doctrine, and the early debates on the interpretation of the Holy Bible during his day. While serving as the head of the school, Pantaenus taught his version of Catholic theology till he died.

Not much is known about the life of Titus Flavius Clemens (a.k.a. Clement of Alexandria). From his writings, we know that he traveled throughout the Roman Empire from Greece to southern Italy, Palestine, and finally Egypt. During his journey Clement converted to Catholicism, but the circumstances of his conversion are unknown. Toward AD 180, Clement met Pantaenus in Alexandria, Egypt. Soon after this happened, Clement took up his permanent residence in

Alexandria, and he became Pantaenus's disciple. After Pantaenus died in AD 200, Clement became the head of the Catechetical School of Alexandria. We also know that Clement, like the other Catholic Church fathers before him, was heavily influenced by Greek philosophy and Platonism. So when he came in contact with Catholicism, he naturally embraced the idea of three divine persons making up one God. We know this because of Clement's writings, which he wrote before and after he became the head of the catechetical school.

From his writings (titled *Protrepticus*, *Paedagogus*, and *Stromata*), we are able to understand the mind of Clement and how he has contributed to the development of the doctrine of the Trinity. For example, the following statement was made by the author who wrote an online article about Clement on Religionfacts.com:

> From a theological point of view, one of the chief aims of Clement was to determine the relations between faith and reason and to show what philosophy has achieved to prepare the world for Christian Revelation and how it must be used in order to transform the data of this revelation into a scientific theology.

Clement, like his teacher Pantaenus, thought that Greek philosophy was a good thing. In fact, Clement emphasized the importance of philosophy in attaining the fullness of Christian knowledge throughout his life. He even sharply criticized those who were unwilling to make any use of philosophy. So instead of asking God to help him to understand His Word, Clement tried to establish Catholic theology by teaching the Logos doctrine according to his understanding of it.

From philosophy Clement takes his conception of the Logos, the principle of Christian gnosis, through whom alone God's relation to the world and His revelation is maintained. This led Clement to teach that the Logos is most closely one with the Father, whose power He resumes in Himself. Also, Clement believed that both the Son and the Spirit are "first-born powers and first created." According to him they form the highest stages in the scale of intelligent being. Clement also distinguishes the Son-Logos from the Logos, who is immutably immanent in God the Father. He even tried to describe philosophy as a direct operation of the Logos. For example, an online encyclopedia article about Clement stated that he taught the following:

> The body of Christ was not subject to human needs. He is the good Physician; the medicine which he offers is the communication of saving *gnosis*, leading men from paganism to faith and from faith to the higher state of knowledge. This true philosophy includes within itself the freedom from sin and the attainment of virtue.

It's obvious that he believes that Christianity is the true philosophy, but Clement's doctrine is similar to Docetism (a Gnostic doctrine that teaches that Christ didn't have a physical body). Clement does admit that Christ had a real body, but he taught that his body was exempt from the common needs of life such as eating and drinking. He even believed that the soul of Christ was exempt from the movement of passions, joy, and of sadness. Once again, Clement and others like him did not understand the dual nature of the Messiah, Jesus. Lastly, Clement recommended a vegetarian diet because he claimed that the apostles Peter, Matthew, and James the Just were vegetarians.

Throughout his life in the third century, Clement had to close the catechetical school because of the great persecution of Emperor Severus. After he closed the school, Clement went to Cappadocia and resided there with one of his disciples. When Emperor Severus died, it is very probable that Clement went back to Alexandria, reopened the catechetical school, and resumed his role as the school's head. Clement continued to write, but his other works were not of any significance. Overall, Clement taught things that are contrary to the word of God, and he wasn't an effective teacher. Even the *Catholic Encyclopedia* states the following about Clement: "He was careful to go to Holy Scripture for his doctrine; but he misused the text by his faulty exegesis." Clement read all the New Testament books except for 2 Peter and 3 John. But due to the fact that he refused to let go of Greek philosophy, Clement was never able to come to the knowledge of the truth. Clement fell asleep as a Catholic in AD 215.

After Clement's death, Origen (AD 185–254) succeeded him as the head of the Catechetical School of Alexandria. He was a student of Clement and a gifted writer. Origen learned the doctrine of the Trinity from Clement, but he would later teach his own version of it. Christian scholar David K. Bernard wrote the following:

> Origen attempted to fuse Greek philosophy and Christianity into a system of higher knowledge that historians often describe as Christian Gnosticism. He accepted the Greek Logos doctrine (namely that the Logos was a person separate from the Father), but he added a unique feature not proposed until his time. This was the doctrine of the eternal Son.

Origen's doctrine of the eternal Son states that the Logos was a separate person from all eternity; the Son was begotten from all eternity and is eternally being begotten. Also, Origen taught that the Son was subordinate to God the Father in existence. (Later on in his life, Origen moved closer to the doctrine of coequality among the persons of the Trinity.) Origen believed that all three persons of the Trinity were fully divine. In addition to these false teachings, Origen taught doctrines that are completely heretical. For example, Origen believed in the preexistence of the souls of men, denied the necessity of the redemptive work of Jesus Christ, and believed in the ultimate salvation of the wicked. He even believed that the devil will be saved by God. But despite these heretical teachings, Origen's understanding of the Father, the Logos, and the Holy Spirit will become essential in the Catholic Church's expression of its teaching on the Trinity a century later.

Novatian (AD 200–258) was one of the first Catholics to emphasize the Holy Spirit as the third person of the Trinity. But his point of view on the Holy Spirit was not embraced by the Catholic Church during his time. Also, Novatian taught that the Son was subordinate to God the Father. He is another Catholic who didn't ask God to help him properly understand His Holy Bible. But Novatian's teaching on the Trinity is not his legacy to the Catholic Church. So I will talk about him some more later on in this chapter.

While all this chaos was happening within the Roman Catholic Church, God's original and primitive ekklesia con-tinued to increase in number throughout the known world. Also, prominent leaders within the messianic community arose and taught the same doctrine of Christ that is in the Holy Bible. These apostolic leaders are the following: Noetus, Praxeas, Epigonus, Cleomenes, and Sabellius. These men were active in the church of God during the last decades of the second century and the first half of the third century. They're some of the saints that God used to win souls and cause His ekklesia to flourish within the Roman Empire.

Noetus was a native of Asia Minor who, at some point in his life, got saved and became the head of his own church in Smyrna. After being converted to faith, he taught the doctrine of the Messiah according to the Scriptures throughout the rest of his life. In fact, Noetus is the reason why his Catholic opponents invented the terms Modalistic Monarchian and Patripassian. For example, Noetus and his followers were called Modalistic Monarchians because they taught that God's Spirit can take on many modes (i.e., Father, Son of God, Holy Spirit, etc.). Also, he claimed to be a true believer of the *One* true God who is king. This King is Jesus the Messiah, who is God the Father manifest in the flesh. But it was the masculine humanity of Christ that died on the cross, not the divinity of the Messiah (the Holy Spirit). Noetus also said, "Jesus was the Son by reason of His birth, but He was also the Father." After being rejected by some Catholics in Asia Minor because of his doctrine, Noetus died some time after AD 220.

Praxeas got saved and became a student of Noetus during the second century. While he was with his teacher, Praxeas became well-versed in the gospel of Christ and biblical doctrines of God. And after suffering some trials and tribulations, Praxeas traveled to Rome, Italy. He was received by the churches there because the ekklesia was almost everywhere. This happened during the nineties of the second century.

God used Praxeas to cause many souls to be born again of the water and of the Spirit. And during his ministry, Praxeas came in contact with Tertullian. The *Catholic Encyclopedia* states the following:

> He was well received at Rome (c. 190- 98) by the pope (Victor, or possibly Zephyrinus). The latter pope had decided to acknowledge the prophetic gifts of Montanus, Prisca, and Maximilla (if we may believe Tertullian). The intention had been sufficiently public to bring peace to the Churches of Asia and Phrygia—so much depended on the papal sanction; but Praxeas prevailed upon the pope to recall his letter.

This decision by the Roman Bishop enraged Tertullian. Also, it is one of the several reasons why Tertullian left the Catholic Church. And when he officially left the Catholic Church and joined the New Prophecy, Tertullian wrote a letter to refute the teachings of Praxeas. Tertullian wrote the following:

> The simple, indeed (I will not call them unwise and unlearned), who always constitute the majority of believers, are startled at the dispensation (of the Three in One), on the very ground that their very Rule of Faith withdraws them from the world's plurality of gods to the one only true God; not understanding that, although He is the one only God, He must yet be believed in with his own economy. The numerical order and distribution of the Trinity, they assume to be a division of the Unity.

Tertullian himself states that the ekklesia outnumbered those who believed in the Trinity. He also states that he was rejected by the saints. Why? He was rejected because his doctrine is foreign to the Holy Bible. Sometime later, in the last decades of his life, Praxeas left Rome and went to Carthage to preach the gospel of God. While in Carthage, God used Praxeas and other members of the ekklesia to convert many Montanists over to the faith. Tertullian didn't like this, but you can't stop God. Praxeas continued to preach the gospel of Jesus until he died. The date of Praxeas's death is unknown.

Epigonus was also a disciple of Noetus. According to Dr. Adolf Harnack, Epigonus came to Rome during the time of Roman Bishop Victor I or Zephyrinus. During his ministry, Epigonus met a man named Cleomenes. He got saved and became Epigonus's disciple. Also, Epigonus evangelized and caused many souls to be baptized in the name of Jesus Christ, and God filled them with the Holy Ghost. He taught the apostle's doctrine till the day he fell asleep in the Lord.

Much of what we know about Cleomenes comes from one of the writings of Hippolytus. He stated that Cleomenes started a theology school in Rome. Hippolytus wrote, "The school of these heretics during the succession of such Bishops, continued to acquire strength and augmentation from the fact that Zephyrinus and Callistus helped them to prevail." And according to Dr. Harnack, Cleomenes headed this theological school until he fell asleep in AD 215.

Sabellius of Libya got saved and became active within the messianic community in Rome. But he really emerged on the scene in AD 215 when he became the head of the theological school that was started by Cleomenes. Sabellius preached the gospel of Elohim and taught the doctrine of the Messiah. The Catholics in Rome called his doctrine Sabellianism, and they didn't like it because of its biblical views. David K. Bernard wrote the following about Sabellius:

> Sabellius relied heavily upon Scripture, especially passages such as Exodus 20:3, Deuteronomy 6:4, Isaiah 44:6, and John 10:38. He said that God revealed Himself as Father in creation, Son in incarnation, Holy Ghost in regeneration and sanctification.

So it was Sabellius who coined this truthful statement about the Lord Jesus Christ. Throughout his life and ministry, Sabellius preached the gospel and taught the doctrine of God according to the Scriptures. And because of his preaching, many pagans believed on the Lord and were baptized as well. The date of Sabellius's death is unknown.

In addition to these holy men of God, the Celts took the apostle's doctrine to ancient Languedoc, Flanders, Frisia, and Saxony. During the twenties of this century, the ekklesia was in Eurasia, Asia, and all over North Africa. The doctrine of the Messiah was in ancient China during and after the Han Dynasty (BC 206–AD 220) . Also, a man named Mani from Persia emerged on the scene. He was born again in Persia, and then he taught the apostle's doctrine. Mani baptized sinners in the name of Jesus, and then the Lord filled them with the Holy Ghost. He also kept the Feast of Pentecost. The date of his death is unknown as well.

While the churches were flourishing in the Roman world and beyond, the Roman Empire almost collapsed on itself. This period of time is called the "Crisis of the Third Century" (AD 235–285). The Roman Empire was having economic, military, and political problems since the second century. But things came to a boiling point during the third century. Hugh Kramer wrote the following in his online article:

> In 235 Ce, things really started to hit the fan when the emperor Severus Alexander was murdered by soldiers incited to mutiny by a general named Maximinus who then took his place. This was the start of 50 years of near unceasing civil wars and emergencies. The soldiers of different frontier

armies began nominating their own generals for the throne. It didn't matter whether the general actually wanted the throne or not. Once nominated, you had no choice but to try and take it.

This was actually happening. The nominated general had to try to take the emperor's throne or be killed by his own soldiers. And if the soldiers didn't kill their own general, then the current Roman Emperor would try to kill him. In fact, thirty emperors reigned during this fifty-year period. But of that number, only two died in their own bed. The rest were assassinated or murdered while Emperor Gordian I committed suicide. There was little to no security for any emperor of this period.

The ekklesia of God suffered persecution during this crisis. This occurred when Emperor Maximinus (AD 235–238) initiated a persecution during the first year of his reign. Anyone who openly confessed to being a Christian and refused to worship the gods of Rome would be imprisoned and put to death. As a result, many saints died during this period, especially the heads of the Catholic Church. They suffered the most during this persecution.

Trajan Decius (AD 249–251) saw Christianity as the enemy of the empire. He called Christians atheists because of their refusal to worship the gods of Rome. According to Samson Hutagalung, Decius said, "Their atheism was responsible for the many troubles in the realm." So because of his hatred toward Christians, Decius initiated a persecu-tion against the saints and Catholics that spanned the entire empire. He is remembered for being one of the cruelest persecutors of Christians. A lot of saints were killed dur-ing this persecution. In fact, Decius had many saints and Catholics killed for entertainment in the Roman Colosseum. Fortunately, this persecution did end a few months before Decius was killed in battle against the Goths. In addition, the messianic community suffered more persecution during the reigns of Emperor Valerian (AD 253–260) and Emperor Aurelian (AD 270–275). And when the persecution under Aurelian ended, the saints of God, along with the Roman citizens, still had to endure what was going on in the empire during this crisis. This fifty-year period was a perilous time for the saints and everyone else in the Roman Empire.

The empire itself was under constant military threat because of their civil wars. For example, the Parthian Empire collapsed in AD 224, but it was replaced by the Persian Empire that posed a constant threat to the eastern part of the Roman Empire. Also, the Goths threatened the northern frontier of the empire. Even separatist states emerged in Gaul and Palmyra, which seriously brought into question the unity of the empire. And due to the constant civil wars within the Roman Empire, their financial system collapsed. The empire itself was reduced to bartering for goods and services. Realistically speaking, the Roman Empire should have collapsed on itself, but it didn't. The costs were great, but the actions taken by Emperors Aurelian and Diocletian (AD 284–305) were monumental. For instance, Aurelian reunited the eastern and western parts of the Roman Empire, and he caused the Roman currency of his day to be put back into circulation. This ended the empire's bartering system. And Diocletian's economic reforms completed the recovery of the empire's economy. In fact, Diocletian is the emperor who established the tetrarchy, which divided the empire into four regions to be ruled by a co-emperor. This tetrarchy split the Roman Empire into two parts: east and west. Diocletian and Galerius ruled in the east while Constantius Chlorus (AD 305–306) and Maximian (AD 286–305) ruled in the west. This happened in AD 293. Diocletian split the Roman Empire, but it would not become an empire with a permanent east and west till after the death of Emperor Theodosius I in the late fourth century. The Roman Empire of the past may have been gone forever, but it will continue to rule the known world for the next two hundred years.

During the fifties of this century, things were not well within the Catholic Church. First of all, Emperor Decius initiated a persecution against all Christians in early AD 250. Soon after this happened, Fabian

(AD 236–250), the bishop of the Roman Church, was killed along with many other Catholics. But a lot of Catholics chose to offer sacrifices to the Roman gods to save their lives while other Catholics fled for their lives to avoid being killed. So when the persecution ended in AD 251, a lot of Catholics who offered sacrifices and fled to avoid martyrdom wanted to rejoin the Roman Church. But some of the clergymen of the Roman Church had severe issues regarding this matter.

The Catholic Church was completely divided regarding those who lapsed during the persecution of Decius. The two parties couldn't agree on what to do with them. An online ency-clopedia article about Bishop Cornelius states the following:

> One side, led by Novatian who was a priest in the diocese of Rome, believed that those who had stopped practicing Christianity during the persecution could not be accepted back into the church even if they repented. Under this philosophy, the only way to reenter the church would be rebaptism. The opposing side, including Cornelius and Cyprian the Bishop of Carthage, did not believe in the need for rebaptism. Instead they thought that the sinners should only need to show contrition and true repentance to be welcomed back into the church.

Now despite these men's differences of opinion, those who lapsed but wanted to rejoin the Catholic Church were received back into it. But soon after, in Carthage, Cyprian himself refused absolution to Catholics who lapsed except in the case of mortal sickness. Doing this did not put the issue to rest. So in order to resolve this issue, Cyprian called a council of North African bishops at Carthage in AD 251 to consider the treatment of the lapsed and the apparent schism of Felicissimus.

The bishops at the council decided that those who had taken part in heathen sacrifices could be received back into the Catholic Church only when on the point of death. They also practiced absolution, which is the priests deciding and declaring when a penitent's sins are forgiven. Apparently, they had forgotten that only God can forgive a person's sins. But I do give them some credit because about a year after they made this crazy-insane decision, this regulation was essentially mitigated at another council in the summer of 252. The Catholics who lapsed were restored if they repented immediately after a sudden fall and eagerly sought absolution. But the clergymen who had fallen were to be deposed and could not be restored to their functions. Meanwhile, back in Rome, Novatian refused absolution to all who had lapsed. But this isn't the only thing that Novatian did during this period.

In AD 251, Cornelius was elected to be the bishop of the Roman Catholic Church. The majority of the clerics accepted his election. But Novatian was very angry that the Roman Church chose Cornelius to be the bishop. In fact, he believed that he was supposed to be the next bishop of Rome. So Novatian became Cornelius's biggest rival by proclaiming himself the antipope (or rival bishop); this caused the second schism within the Catholic Church. An online encyclopedia article about Novatian states the following:

> Novatian had hoped to be elected and accused Cornelius of foul play. He then summoned three bishops from the remote corners of Italy to come to Rome as fast as possible, along with the other bishops, to mediate on an internal division. These simple men were forced to make Novatian a bishop at 10 am…To ensure his supporters' loyalty Novatian forced them to swear on the consecrated bread and wine at Holy Communion that they would not go back over to Cornelius.

After this happened, both Cornelius and Novatian rushed to send out their messengers to the Catholic churches to announce their election. This was a soap opera for real. Then in October of 251, Cornelius called a council of sixty bishops and had Novatian excommunicated from the Catholic Church. As a result, Novatian founded his own group of

Catholics called the Novatianists. Also, he continued to serve as the rival bishop of the Catholic Church after the death of Cornelius in AD 253.

Throughout the rest of his life, Novatian continued to teach heretical doctrines, including emphasizing the Holy Ghost as the third person of the Trinity. But he believed that only God can forgive a person's sins and not the Roman Church. So Novatian was labeled a heretic by the Catholic Church. The schismatic church that Novatian established continued for the next several centuries after his death in AD 258.

There was another issue that was irritating the Catholic Church: The saints of Elohim baptizing sinners in the name of Jesus the Messiah. God's ekklesia was everywhere throughout the known world, and the Catholic Church was severely outnumbered by them. And in AD 255, this was the case in North Africa, including Carthage. So in response to God's ekklesia immersing sinners into the name of Jesus, Cyprian, the Catholic bishop of Carthage, made a change to the Trinitarian formula of baptism. As I explained to you earlier, the original Catholic formula of baptism was a triple immersion. In fact, the second baptism was usually done in the name of Jesus Christ. So due to the fact that the ekklesia and the Catholics had this one thing in common, Cyprian took out the name of Jesus and replaced it with the title "Son." And by doing this, Cyprian and his followers were only repeating the instruction of the Lord rather than obeying His command.

Now the Roman Catholics knew that the Acts of the Apostles only taught water baptism into the name of Jesus Christ. But during this time, the Catholics were two-God people. In other words, they believed in God the Father and Jesus the Son. They believed in the Holy Ghost, but the Spirit was not universally recognized as deity or the third person of the Trinity. Also, they believed that the Father is not the Son and the Son is not the Father. So if you baptize someone in the name of Jesus, then this means that Jesus is the Father, Son, and Holy Spirit. Hence, there is no Trinity. Cyprian and the rest of the Catholic Church understood this very well. So instead of humbling himself and being baptized the New Testament way, Cyprian became more stubborn and antichrist by taking the name of Jesus out of an already false formula of baptism.

Stephen I (AD 254–257), the bishop of the Roman Catholic Church, did not agree with Cyprian and the Catholic churches in Carthage. The *Encyclopedia Britannica* states the following:

> In the third century baptism in the name of Christ was still so widespread that Pope Stephen, in opposition to Cyprian of Carthage, declared it to be valid.

In the *New Catholic Encyclopedia*, scholar J. A. Jungmann wrote the following:

> Though there is no clear proof that this phrase was really used as a liturgical formula, the possibility of its being used thus even as late as the third century cannot be excluded (Stenzel 88–93) . After all, the validity of Baptism "in the name of Jesus" was still accepted in the age of scholasticism.

Now Bishop Stephen I believed in and practiced the Catholic formula of baptism. But because of the Acts of the Apostles and the baptism in the name of Jesus Christ being so widespread, he declared the biblical formula of baptism to be valid as well. And according to Christian scholar Harry A. Peyton, Stephen I believed in the divine power that is in the name of Jesus. In fact, Stephen believed that anyone who has been baptized in the name of Jesus has obtained the remission of sins, even outside of the Catholic Church.

Stephen took action against Cyprian for taking the name of Jesus out of their Trinitarian formula of baptism. Harry A. Peyton wrote the following:

> In 255 AD, Cyprian called a Council at Carthage in which 31 bishops denounced baptism in the name of Jesus. This

is the first council in history, where baptism in the name of Jesus was formally denounced. After this Council, Catholic Pope Stephen called a Roman Council, in which he and other Catholic Bishops excommunicate Cyprian and all those in the African Synod for their stand on baptism.

Cyprian could care less because the majority of the North African bishops sided with him. And in the following year, Cyprian wrote letters to other Catholics who agreed with him. He even gained the support of the Eastern Catholics churches by gaining the support of Firmilian, bishop of Caesarea. In one of his letters, Cyprian wrote the following:

> How, therefore do some say that a Gentile baptized without, outside the Church, nay rather, and against the [Catholic] Church, provided it be in the Name of Jesus Christ, wherever it be and whatever it be, can obtain the remission of sins, when Christ Himself ordered the gentiles to be baptized in the complete and united Trinity.

Now it's obvious that the last part of his statement is utterly false. But what he's trying to say is this: If the baptism of the ekklesia is correct, then they are children of God just like the Catholics. And since the beliefs and doctrines of the ekklesia are so different from the Catholic Church, Cyprian believes that this can't be true. Also, he believes that baptism in the name of Jesus cannot be the true baptism of the New Testament. Only the Catholic formula of baptism is correct in his heart.

Prior to Bishop Stephen's death in AD 257, he learned that the Catholic churches in the east were rebaptizing heretics, particularly the Montanists who wanted to join the Catholic Church. Because of these acts, Stephen I excommunicated the eastern Catholic churches. Then he was killed during the persecution of Emperor Valerian. And in the following year, Cyprian was also killed during this persecution. Cyprian's legacy is this: He was the first Catholic to use the title "Son" when baptizing someone into the Trinity with three immersions. This was not popular within the Catholic Church during his time. But as time went on, all clerics within the Roman Church will take the name of Jesus out of their baptism and substitute God's name with "Son."

Now before I move on, I must tell you some of the other things that the Catholic Church did during this century. For instance, penance was enforced. This is a Roman Catholic sacrament in which a sinner had to be punished by going before the clergy and openly show how sorry he/she is for committing a certain sin. In other words, sinners had to openly embarrass themselves in front of the clerics. And after the sinner confessed his/her sins to the priest, the priest would forgive that person's sins and declare his/her freedom from the punishment of sin. This is also the Catholic sacrament of absolution. Catholic clerics believed that they had the divine authority to forgive a person's sin. So within the Catholic Church, biblical repentance was completely thrown out. In addition, at the Council of Carthage in AD 252, they decided that all newborn infants must be baptized within eight days. And just in case you didn't know, infant baptism is not biblical!

Throughout the rest of the third century, all things pretty much remained the same within the Roman Catholic Church. They baptized new converts three times into the Trinity, they partook of the Eucharist, and their clerics practiced their so-called authority to forgive a person's sins. The Catholic Church continued to elect bishops to be the head of their church. Also, the doctrine of the Trinity was still incomplete, and the Catholics were continuing to have problems with it. For example, was the Holy Spirit divine or not? A solution to this problem would not be found until the next century.

There were thousands of preachers in the ekklesia during the second half of the third century. But only a few of them are known in world history. One of them was a saint named Commodian. Very little is known about him. All that we know is that he was born again of the water and of the Spirit during the first half of the third century. Then in

AD 250, Commodian became the bishop of his own church somewhere in North Africa. In his book titled *A History of Oneness throughout the Centuries*, Harry A. Peyton wrote the following:

> According to Harvard professor Harry A. Wolfson, in his work entitled The Philosophy Of The Church Fathers, Commodian taught in verse 91 of his Carmen Apologeticum: the Father went into the Son, at Bethlehem. This revealed that the Father was the God who was in the Lord Jesus Christ. He also added: Commodian speaking for himself, says almost in the words quoted above [i.e. God is only one person] as representing the views of Praxeas and Noetus."

So Commodian's doctrine was viewed to be similar to the doctrine that was taught by Noetus and Praxeas. Commodian also preached the good news of Jesus the Messiah according to the Scriptures. As a result, his enemies labeled him a Patripassian. Throughout his life, Commodian preached Jesus till the day that he fell asleep in the Lord. This is all that is known about him. The date of his death is unknown.

Paul of Samosata (AD 200–275) was a man of humble beginnings. According to Christian scholar Marvin M. Arnold, he was an ex-Catholic. But the year of his conversion to true Christianity is unknown. In AD 260, Paul was elected bishop of Antioch. Also, he held the civil office of procurator *ducenarius* and was protected by Zenobia, the famous queen of Palmyra ruling in Syria. Paul taught the doctrine of the Messiah. Because of his teachings, he was not popular among the Catholics in the east. An online encyclopedia article about Paul states the following:

> He aroused controversy with his Monarchianist teachings. In 269, seventy bishops, priests and deacons assembled at Antioch as a synod. They deposed Paul as bishop and elected Dominus as his successor.

Paul suffered persecution because of his teachings, but he held on to what God had revealed to him. Nobody knows for sure what he did during the last years of his life. But I believe that Paul served God till he took his last breath.

Mamas of Cappadocia came on the scene during the sixties and seventies of this century. Very little is known about him. All that we know is this: Mamas preached the gospel of Yeshua according to the Scriptures, and he taught the apostle's doctrine. And according to Christian Historian Marvin M. Arnold, Mamas died at the hands of his Catholic opponents.

The rest of the ekklesia of God continued to increase in number throughout known world, including the nations far beyond the Roman Empire. But the most interesting fact is this: God's original and primitive ekklesia constantly irritated the Roman Catholic Church in the east and west. The saints were not doing this on purpose. God was just doing His job by dealing with and leading many members of the Catholic Church away from the Catholic religion unto the knowledge of the truth. In other words, Elohim caused many Catholics to embrace the truth and be baptized in the name of Jesus the Messiah, and Jesus filled them with the Holy Ghost. And despite the spread of Catholicism within the Roman Empire, the Catholics were severely outnumbered by God's messianic community. And every time they tried to bring their doctrines into the churches of Yeshua, they were rejected. God's ekklesia was triumphant. And at the end of the third century, the saints of God were waiting on the coming of the Lord as they entered into the fourth century.

THE FOURTH CENTURY

The more things change, the more they stay the same. I say this because things were at least okay for the churches of God during the first few years of the fourth century. In fact, the ekklesia enjoyed a time of peace during most of the years of Diocletian's reign. But in the year AD 303, Emperor Diocletian initiated what is now called the Great Persecution against all who claimed to be followers of Christ. This was the worst of all the persecutions that the ekklesia had to endure in the Roman Empire. The following events occurred:

> On February 23, 303 AD the cathedral in Nicomedia was torn down. The next day an imperial edict was issued ordering all Christian church buildings to be destroyed, all sacred writings were to be surrendered to authorities to be burned, all sacred items used in Christian meetings were to be confiscated, and worship meetings were outlawed.

This was only the beginning. The author of this online article also wrote the following:

Just a few months later another edict was issued ordering the arrest of all clergy—so many were arrested that they had to halt arrests due to the overflowing of the prisons. In early 304 all Christians were required to make sacrifice to the empire on the pain of death.

Things were getting worse and worse for the messianic community in many regions of the empire. Countless saints of God and Catholics died during Diocletian's reign. The emperor even caused many saints and Catholics to die in the Colosseum and other arenas throughout the Roman Empire.

In AD 305, Diocletian resigned as emperor due to illness and was succeeded by Galerius (AD 305–311). After this happened, the Great Persecution against God's elect and the Catholics intensified, especially in the east. The Romans used their evil imaginations to kill the saints of God in many ways. The churches were either imprisoned, set on fire, crucified, fed to wild beasts, tortured, killed with swords, or poisoned. Many saints lost their personal property. They even used famine to try to kill off the ekklesia. Many Catholics were killed as well. And when Galerius died in AD 311, the Great Persecution continued for two more years.

This persecution against Elohim's churches was horrible, but it could've been worse. For instance, the author of the online article "Diocletian and the Great Persecution" wrote the following:

> While the anti-Christian edicts issued by Diocletian and Galerius were meant to be empire wide, the persecution in the west seems to have been confined to some churches being pulled down by Constantius in Gaul, Britain and Spain and no one was executed. Even the obvious Christians in Rome were not arrested in the early years of the persecution suggesting that even the Augustus, Maximian did not enforce the edict, although he may later have used it as an excuse to confiscate land for himself.

The fact that the Great Persecution was executed in this way in the western part of the empire is nothing but the grace of God. Nevertheless, the saints of God who resided in the eastern part of the empire suffered more persecution than the saints in the west. And when you compare the number of Christian and Catholic martyrs to the number of Jews that died during the Bar-Kokhba Revolt, the number of saints and Catholics that died is small. Like I said, it could've been worse.

The Great Persecution against all Christians and Catholics finally ended in AD 313. This is when Emperor Constantine I (AD 306–337) issued the Edict of Milan, which proclaimed religious tolerance of all religions throughout the Roman Empire. Constantine returned everything that God's elect and the Catholics had lost during the persecution, including church buildings. Also, he removed all penalties for professing to be a follower of Christ. Even Constantine himself converted to Catholicism shortly after issuing this edict (even though he refused to be baptized) . This edict also offered protection from religious persecution for all religious groups. This edict changed everything for the ekklesia and Catholics in the empire. The saints of Yeshua were now free to openly worship God with the protection of the empire. There were minor forms of persecution against the ekklesia and Catholics in the east prior to the Council of Nicaea, but the Great Persecution itself was over.

These are the events that occurred and are significant in world history: Constantine I became the emperor of the west when his father Constantius died in AD 306. Several years later, Constantine formed an alliance with co-emperor Licinius I (AD 308–324). He did this by giving his half sister to Licinius in marriage. Also, both emperors came together and agreed to end the Great Persecution in AD 313. When this happened, things were peaceful within the messianic and Catholic communities, right? Wrong! Things were peaceful in the messianic community. But in the so-called Christian communities such as the Roman Catholics and Donatists, there was chaos. The Catholics were still struggling to lay the foundation of their Trinitarian doctrine, and there was a schism going on in Africa because of the Donatists. So after Constantine issued the Edict of Milan, he would soon inherit an empire that was in religious disarray.

Constantine did a lot of things during his reign as emperor of the west. This is especially true in regards to what happened during and after the Great Persecution. For instance, many Catholics in Africa gave up their copies of the Holy Bible to be publicly burned by the Romans. The following event occurred:

> At the consecration of bishop Caecilian of Carthage in 311, one of the three bishops, Felix, bishop of Aptunga, who consecrated Caecilian, had given copies of the Bible to the Roman persecutors. A group of about 70 bishops formed a synod and declared the consecration of the bishop to be invalid. Great debate arose concerning the validity of the sacraments (baptism, the Lord's Supper, etc.) by one who had sinned so greatly against other Christians.

In addition to this, some Catholic Church leaders betrayed other Catholics by snitching on and turning them over to the Romans. Now that's what I call betrayal. These Catholic Church leaders and others like them were called *traditores*, which means "people who had handed over." And when the Great Persecution ended, the following event occurred:

> These traditors had returned to positions of authority under Constantine I, and the Donatists proclaimed that any sacraments celebrated by these priests and bishops were invalid.

These things caused the situation in North Africa to heat up. After the death of Caecilian, Donatus Magnus became bishop of Carthage. The Donatists were eventually named after him.

The primary disagreement between the Donatists and the Catholic Church was over the treatment of those who renounced their faith during the persecution. The Donatists and the Catholics had opposing views on this issue, especially when it came to the rights of those people to partake in church sacraments (i.e., the Eucharist, confession). Even the right to go back to church was debated. An online encyclopedia article on Donatism states the following:

> The orthodox Catholic position was that…the Church still followed the discipline of public penance whereby a penitent for such a grievous offence would spend years, even decades, first outside the doors of the church begging for the prayers of those entering, then kneeling inside the church building during services, then standing with the congregation, and finally receiving the Eucharist again in a long progress toward full reconciliation. The Donatists held that such a crime, after the forgiveness of Baptism, disqualified one for leadership in the Church, a position of extreme rigorism.

Wow! Not even God treats the worst of sinners the way the Catholic Church treated them. On the other hand, the Donatists believed that any clergyman who lapsed during the Great Persecution should not have the right to be restored to leadership in the church ever again. And all sacraments performed by these priests are invalid. Now here's where it gets interesting.

According to the Catholics, it doesn't matter if a clergyman is living a holy lifestyle with clean hands. As long as he has made himself available to God to be used by Him, he can serve as bishop, pastor, or some other leader in the church. An online encyclopedia article on Donatism also states the following:

> The Catholic position…was ex opere operato—*from the work having been worked*; in other words, that the validity of the sacrament depends upon the holiness of God, the

> minister being a mere instrument of God's work, so that any priest or bishop, even one in a state of mortal sin, who speaks the formula of the sacrament with valid matter and the intent of causing the sacrament to occur acts validly.

So by this time, holiness was not a priority in the Catholic Church. The two opposing parties were getting nowhere at resolving their issues. As a result, many towns with large Donatist and Catholic communities were divided between the two. But at the same time, the Donatists were increasing in number throughout North Africa. This posed a slight problem for the Catholic Church.

Since the Donatists and Catholics were not getting anywhere close to resolving their issues, Constantine got involved in the dispute and called the Council of Arles in AD 314. The issues between the two were debated. After the Donatists made their appeal to the secular power, the final decisions that were made at the council were against the Donatists. An online encyclopedia article about the council states the following:

> It excommunicated Donatus and passed twenty-two canons concerning Easter (which should be held on the same day throughout the world, rather than being set by each local church), against the non- residence of clergy, against participation in races and gladiatorial fights (to be punished by excommunication), against the rebaptism of heretics, and on other matters of discipline. Clergymen who could be proven to have delivered sacred books in persecution (the traditores) should be deposed, but their official acts were to be held valid.

Not only was Donatus and his followers excommunicated by the Catholic Church, the Donatists became enemies of the Roman Church and the authorities. For example, in AD 317, Constantine sent troops to deal with the Donatists in Carthage. So the Catholics, who had come out of persecution, were now persecuting the Donatists. This decision by the emperor resulted in banishments but ultimately failed. So Constantine withdrew his troops and ended the persecutions in AD 321. The Donatist church, which also drew their beliefs from the writings of Cyprian and Tertullian, survived to about the seventh century.

While Constantine was dealing with the Donatist schism, a man named Arius (AD 256–336) came on the scene. Arius was a popular preacher and presbyter from Libya who was given pastoral duties in Alexandria, Egypt. He caused the Arian controversy, which began because of a disagreement between him and his bishop, Alexander, in AD 318. Their differences centered on how to express the Catholic understanding of God using current philosophical language. As I explained to you in the two previous chapters, the Catholic Church used Greek philosophy to try to understand the Holy Bible. Don Closson states the following in his online article:

> Alexander argued that Scripture presented God the Father and Jesus as having an equally eternal nature. Arius felt that Alexander's comments supported a heretical view of God called Sabellianism which taught that the Son was merely a different mode of the Father rather than a different person.

Alexander was Catholic. But whenever you quote the Holy Scriptures literally and use them to describe who God is, you will sound like a true Christian. A broken clock is right twice a day. But both of these men heard of and rejected sound doctrine. Arius not only believed that Jesus Christ was subordinate to the Father, he taught that the Son was of an inferior substance in a metaphysical sense. In other words, the Son was inferior to the Father rather than equal. Also, Arius taught that the Son had a beginning. Arius's doctrine was a major threat to the belief that the Father and the Son are both equal and eternal.

What started off as a disagreement between two clerics became a huge movement lead by Arius. The numbers of Arius's followers increased dramatically over the next few years. This happened because Alexander didn't act quickly enough to suppress Arius's teachings. Alexander did call a local council, and those who attended the council decided to excommunicate Arius. But it was too late. An online encyclopedia article on Arius states the following:

> By the time Bishop Alexander finally acted against his recalcitrant presbyter, Arius's doctrine had spread far beyond his own see; it had become a topic of discussion—and disturbance—for the entire Church.

After he was excommunicated, Arius left Africa and traveled through Palestine and Asia Minor in ancient Turkey. Arianism increased in those parts of the Roman Empire as well.

Arius was kindly received by Eusebius of Caesarea (AD 263–339), Eusebius of Nicomedia, and many other bishops of the eastern Catholic churches. In fact, many of these Catholic churches favored Arius's doctrine. An online article on Arius states the following:

> Arius found powerful friends in Eusebius of Nicomedia, Eusebius of Caesarea, Paulinus of Tyre, Gregory of Berytus, Aetius of Lydda, and other bishops who either shared his view, or at least considered it innocent. He took refuge with Eusebius at Nicomedia, which had been the imperial residence since Diocletian, and spread his views in a half-poetic work, *Thalia* ("The Banquet"), of which Athanasius has preserved fragments.

So because of Arius, Arianism became a bigger problem to the Catholic Church than God's original and primitive ekklesia. And the saints outnumbered both of these groups. As a result of the spread of Arianism in the east, violence between the Arians and Roman Catholics increased. The debates between the Arians and the Catholics that taught *homoousion* (the idea that the Father, Son, and Holy Ghost are of the same exact substance and are coequally God) became so violent that there was bloodshed in many towns.

While all of this was happening, the alliance between Emperors Constantine and Licinius had deteriorated. Like all men of great power, both emperors wanted to be the sole ruler of the Roman Empire. There were many Arians, Catholics, and saints residing in the east. And since Constantine converted to Catholicism, Licinius viewed all who called themselves Christians in the east as a threat to him. So Licinius initiated a persecution against all who proclaimed to be followers of Christ. Many died in the eastern part of the empire. Also, many church buildings and copies of the Holy Bible went up in flames. When Constantine heard of this, his alliance with the co-emperor was officially over.

Constantine used this as an excuse to attack Licinius and his army. He immediately sent troops to march on his eastern rival. Soon, Constantine and his army met Licinius and his army on the battlefield. He drove Licinius and his army back into the east. From ancient Adrianople to Chrysopolis, Constantine pursued his rival. And in AD 324, Constantine and his army annihilated Licinius's army in Chrysopolis. Constantine won sole rulership of the Roman Empire.

Constantine captured Licinius, his brother-in-law, and imprisoned him in Nicomedia. Licinius's wife pleaded with Constantine to spare her husband's life. At first he did, but then Constantine decided to have Licinius executed. Catholics will be Catholics. Afterward, he renamed the city of Byzantium after him by naming it Constantinople, which is located in ancient Turkey. This city became a Catholic city. So all is now well with Constantine's empire, right? Absolutely not! His empire was still in religious disarray because the Arians and Catholics were killing each other in the streets of towns located in the east. There was no unity in Constantine's Roman Empire.

Before I move on, I must bring out this important fact: Constantine giving himself the title Pontifex Maximus, or Supreme Pontiff, was nothing new. Now you're probable thinking, "What is the author of this book talking about?" I'm talking about this title, which is the same title that today's pope, Francis, has. Mark Bonocore states the following in his online article:

> The *early* Church Fathers spoke of the Pontifex Maximus in such derogatory, paganistic ways. Because when the *early* Fathers were writing, the Pontifex Maximus was the head of the Roman *pagan* religion, and the Roman Empire itself was pagan. As any student of Roman history knows, the Pontifex Maximus was an imperial office, usually held by the Emperor himself, which made one the "chief priest" of the Roman "state cult."

Mark Bonocore also wrote the following:

> Now as I said, in the days of the early Fathers, this "state cult" was paganism and Emperor worship. Yet, when Constantine the Great became the first **Christian** Roman Emperor, the "state cult" changed to Christianity. Now, oddly enough, the first Christian emperors all still retained the title of Pontifex Maximus (a traditional title for Emperors) which, under imperial law (though not Church law), actually made them the "Head of the Church"!

That's right! As I said before, the earliest Roman bishops of the Catholic Church were not popes at all. They were just presiding bishops. So the very first pope of the Roman Catholic Church was Emperor Constantine. And the man that served as the Roman Bishop of the Catholic Church during Constantine's reign was Sylvester I (AD 314–335).

Since the Arians and Catholics couldn't solve their theological debate on their own, Constantine used his authority to call the Council of Nicaea to settle the Arian controversy. This council took place in AD 325. It composed of Catholic prelates from all parts of the empire to resolve this issue. Arius and some of his followers attended the council as well. But the majority of the Catholic bishops who attended this council came from the east. Bishop Sylvester I sent two priests as his delegates because he was too aged to attend the council. And there was a saint of God named Marcellus who attended the council. He was the bishop of his own assembly in Ancyra, which is located in ancient Galatia. Also, Constantine was there at the council, and he presided over the whole thing. And the Catholics had someone there to be their champion: a young deacon named Athanasius (AD 296–373).

The Arian and Catholic Church leaders were there to consider one vital question: Was Jesus Christ equal to God the Father, or was He something else? Constantine was no spectator. As the head of the Catholic Church, he participated in and even led some of the discussions. An online encyclopedia article on Arius states the following:

> Twenty-two bishops, led by Eusebius of Nicomedia, came as supporters of Arius. But when some of Arius's writings were read aloud, they are reported to have been denounced as blasphemous by most participants.

This same article also states the following:

> For about two months, the two sides argued and debated, with each appealing to Scripture to justify their respective positions. Arius maintained that the Son of God was a Creature, made from nothing; and that Christ was God's First Production, before all ages. And he argued that everything else was created through the Son. Thus, said Arius, only the Son was directly created and begotten of God; furthermore, there was a time that He had no existence.

Some of the things that Arius said are biblical. But he, like the Catholics, rejected the doctrine of the Messiah that was being taught by the ekklesia. In fact, Marcellus voiced his doctrinal views at the council, and he showed proof that he was against the doctrines of Arianism. But according to the *Catholic Encyclopedia Online*, Marcellus's doctrine was viewed to be the opposite extreme of Arianism. His teachings were labeled modified Sabellianism, which is another name for the biblical doctrine of Christ. So Marcellus had no impact on the council's final decision on the Arian controversy. His presence there was largely unnoticed. But God used Marcellus in a mighty way after the Council of Nicaea. So I will talk about him later on in this chapter.

Athanasius responded to Arius by saying, "If Christ were not truly God, then He could not bestow life upon the repentant and free them from sin and Death." Athanasius also argued, in his own words, that Christ is coequal to God the Father and of the same substance of the Father. The debate between the two sides was heated. In fact, according to many accounts, the debate at the council became so heated that at one point Nicholas of Myra slapped Arius in the face. Imagine being Constantine witnessing all this madness. The emperor didn't care who won the debate; he just wanted one of the two sides to win and come to an agreement so that there would be peace between these two churches.

When the debate on Christ's divinity was concluded, the members of the council decided against the Arians. And under the emperor's influence, the majority of the bishops ultimately agreed upon a creed called the Nicene Creed. In terms of the doctrine of the Trinity, the Nicene Creed states the following:

> We believe in one God, the Father Almighty, maker of heaven and earth, and of all things visible and invisible. And in one Lord Jesus Christ, the only begotten Son of God, and born of the Father before all ages. (God of God) light of light, true God of true God. Begotten not made, consubstantial to the Father, by whom all things were made...And in the Holy Ghost, the Lord and Giver of life, who proceeds from the Father (and the Son), who together with the Father and the

Son is to be adored and glorified, who spoke by the Prophets.
And one holy, catholic, and apostolic Church.

For the first time in world history, the doctrine of the Trinity is defined and written on paper. The Holy Spirit is recognized in this creed, but the Spirit wasn't universally believed on as deity within the Catholic Church. This won't happen till later on in this century.

In addition to the Nicene Creed, the council settled the controversy as to the time of celebrating Easter. In regards to Easter, the Catholic Church decided the following: (1) Easter must be celebrated by all throughout the world on the same Sunday, (2) this Sunday must follow the fourteenth day of the paschal moon, (3) that that moon was to be accounted the paschal moon whose fourteenth day followed the Spring equinox, and (4) that some provision should be made, probably by the Church of Alexandria as best skilled in astronomical calculations, for determining the proper date of Easter and communicating it to the rest of the world. Also, the council dealt with the Meletian schism. And lastly, Arius and some of his supporters were deposed and exiled to Illyricum.

Soon after this happened, Arius took refuge in the Middle East. But several years later, he was permitted by the emperor to return to Alexandria in AD 331. Arius would spend the rest of his life defending his religious views against the Catholic Church till he died suddenly in AD, 336. And after his death, the Arian controversy will continue to be a thorn in the side of the Catholic Church for centuries in parts of the west.

Even though he issued strict orders against Arianism, Constantine vacillated on the views of the opposing parties throughout his reign. He obviously wasn't satisfied with the fact that the council did not end the conflict. He wanted peace within the empire. So according to an online encyclopedia article on Arius, Constantine did the following:

> Constantine gradually became more lenient toward those whom the Council of Nicaea had exiled. Though he never repudiated the council or its decrees, the emperor ultimately permitted Arius (who had taken refuge in Palestine) and many of his adherents to return to their homes, once Arius had reformulated his Christology to mute the ideas found most objec-tionable by his critics.

This same article also states the following:

> The emperor directed Alexander of Constantinople to receive Arius, despite the bishop's objections; Bishop Alexander responded by earnestly praying that Arius might perish before this could happen.

Wow! Now this is what I call drama. Even the online *Catholic Encyclopedia* states that Arius had an interview with Constantine and submitted a creed, which the emperor judged to be orthodox. So the Council of Nicaea did nothing to end the Arian controversy.

History records that Emperor Constantine, throughout the rest of his life, did some other things after the Nicene Council. One of the things he did was having his son Crispus imprisoned and prepared for execution. Crispus was sent to ancient Pola in AD 326. Constantine did this because his second wife falsely accused Crispus of trying to seduce her. This was premeditated. She did this so that her two sons could succeed Constantine as co-emperors. While his son was in Pola, Constantine's mother talked to him and reasoned with him. She convinced her son that his wife was lying to him. After he realized the truth, Constantine had his wife killed. Then he tried to recall his order to have Crispus executed, but it was too late. Crispus was killed with the sword. The guilt of having his own son killed will stay with the emperor for the rest of his life.

Among other things, Constantine built Catholic churches in Jerusalem, Bethlehem, Constantinople, and Rome. The most magnificent of all these church buildings was the original St. Peter's Basilica, which was built in AD 330. During those days, this cathedral was an architectural masterpiece. And in AD 337, Constantine, now old and unwell, finally submitted to baptism. From a rational standpoint, it would make sense for him to delay his baptism for salvation because Roman emperors have to do a lot of nasty and sinful things. But it's too bad that this baptism was into the Father, the Son, and the Holy Spirit instead of into the Lord Jesus. And the fact that he thought that he could do whatever he wants and then do what he thought God says to do at the last minute is a slap to God's face. Perhaps Constantine is one of the reasons why deathbed salvation is so popular among some of today's Christians. Constantine will forever be remembered for merging the Catholic Church with the state of Rome. Before he did this, the majority of Romans believed in and worshipped all the gods of Rome, which are part of the ancient mystery religions. But during Constantine's reign and throughout the rest of this century, the beliefs of the Babylonians, Egyptians, Greeks, Eastern cultures, and Romans will infiltrate Catholicism as the Roman government merges itself with the Catholic Church. This is Constantine's legacy to Roman Catholicism. The emperor fell asleep as a Catholic in AD 337. His sons Constantine II (AD 337–340), Constantius II (AD 337–361), and Constans I (AD 337– 350) succeeded him as co-emperors of the Roman Empire.

The Catholics' victory over Arianism did not last long after the Council of Nicaea ended. Due to the fact that Constantine vacillated on the views of each party, the Arians and Catholics continued to fight each other in various ways. An online article on Arius states the following:

> Arianism now entered the stage of its political power. This was a period of the greatest excitement in Church and State: Council was held against council; creed was set up against creed; anathema was hurled against anathema.

This online article also states the following:

> The churches, the theaters, the hippodromes, the feasts, the markets, the streets, the baths, and the shops of Constantinople and other large cities were filled with dogmatic disputes.

This article is talking about the various synods and other things that occurred during this period. In fact, there are several major councils that will take place between the Arians and Catholics throughout this century. Here's what happened at one of them.

Arianism triumphed over Catholicism at the Council of Tyre in AD 335. As a result of this synod, Athanasius was exiled by Constantine to Trier (located in modern -day Germany). After two and a half years, Athanasius was able to resume his role as bishop of the Alexandrian Catholic Church. Then he was deposed and exiled again by Emperor Constantius II because of the Arians in AD 339. Constantius believed in the doctrines of Arianism. So when he became the emperor, Arianism became the official religion of the Roman Empire. Constantius's reign was a tough period for the Catholic Church. But despite these things being against him, Athanasius will spend the rest of his life leading the conflict against the Arians.

Since the forties of this century, Athanasius spent his life and ministry in and out of exile. He was in a constant seesaw battle with the Arians. In fact, Athanasius was banished five or six times throughout his ministry. This man risked his life to defend what he believed to be the truth. It's just too bad that what he believed is another false way. After decades of quarreling against the Arians, Athanasius fell asleep as a Catholic in AD 373. The things that this man did for the Catholic faith still endures to this very day.

The Catholics were fighting hard to push out and propagate their Nicene Creed. But the Arians were resisting them. It was literally a seesaw battle between the Catholics and the Arians. As a result, intolerance and violence against the Arians increased. And things got worse when Constantine and the emperors that followed him got heavily involved in the conflict between these opposing parties. It was like pouring gasoline into the flames.

While all this chaos was happening, God's ekklesia was increasing in number in Africa, Asia, and Europe. This continued during and after the reign of Emperor Constantine. Miracles of God continued within the ekklesia, and countless sinners who heard the gospel of Christ believed and were baptized. This happened because of the numerous men and women of Elohim who were great preachers of holiness. Little to nothing is known about them except two men. One of them was Wolflein (which means Little Wolf). He was an awesome man of God whose ministry spanned from AD 320–340. According to Christian historian Marvin M. Arnold, Wolflein caused millions among the Indo-European tribes to be baptized in the name of Jesus. God used His saint in a mighty way! The date of Wolflein's death is unknown.

The other man of God was Marcellus of Ancyra. A few years after the Nicene Council, Marcellus wrote a book against Asterius, a prominent Arian. In his work, Marcellus taught the following:

> God was originally only One Personality, but at the creation of the universe the Word or Logos went out from the Father and was God's Activity in the world. This Logos became incarnate in Christ and was thus constituted the Son of God.

Marcellus believed that the Logos is God Himself made known in the flesh. This is sound biblical teaching. And because of the soundness of his doctrine, Marcellus was deposed at Constantinople in AD 336 at a synod under the presidency of Eusebius of Nicomedia. Then the following event occurred:

> Marcellus sought redress at Rome from Julius I, who in the autumn of 340 declared Marcellus innocent of the charges brought against him, and reinstated him in his see.

God was using Marcellus to evangelize the Arians, and many of them became saints because of the gospel of God that he preached. Even Julius I (AD 337–352), the bishop of Rome during this period, declared his teachings to be biblically correct. In addition, Marcellus was in contact with Athanasius. But his relation with Athanasius was perturbed by his doctrinal beliefs of Modalism. And from AD 347 to the end of his life, Marcellus lived in exile because of Emperor Constantius II. Where he spent his life in exile is unknown. Marcellus continued to evangelize and cause many sinners to receive the Holy Spirit till he died in AD 374.

During the second half of the fourth century, the Roman Catholic Church and the Roman Empire changed forever. As I mentioned earlier, Constantine and the Roman Emperors that followed him were also popes of the Catholic Church. But this changed when Emperor Gratian (AD 367–383), the last emperor to hold the title Pontifex Maximus bestowed this title on Roman Bishop Damasus I (AD 366–384). From this point on, Damasus and every Roman bishop after him will exercise rule as the pope of the Roman Catholic Church. In addition, the population of the empire was dwindling. This was happening over time because of the diseases that were foreign to the empire. But how did these diseases (mainly small pox and measles) get in the empire? This happened because of the Roman Empire's success. Since the second century, the empire became very efficient at importing goods from the outside world. As a result, the diseases of the outside world were imported as well.

As the population of the Roman Empire decreased, so did its army. The empire's boarder guard was dwindling as well. While this was happening, there were hostile invaders that were threatening the empire. This caused the empire to recruit foreigners, such as the barbarians, to its army in order to defend its expansive frontiers. And because the Roman Empire was so big, it was divided into two parts in the fourth century. Emperor Valentinian I (AD 364–375) ruled and defended the west in Rome while Emperor Valens (AD 364– 378) defended the east in Constantinople.

Valens was challenged to defend the east in AD 378 when the Goths sacked Adrianople. He and his army marched to Adrianople to fight these barbarian warriors. During the battle, Valens and his army were slaughtered at Adrianople. About two-thirds of the army was lost. And Valens himself was killed on the battlefield.

After this happened, Emperor Theodosius I (AD 379–395) ascended to the throne in the east. During his reign, Theodosius issued decrees that effectively made Roman Catholicism the official state religion of the Roman Empire. Also, the emperor convened the Council of Constantinople in AD 381. Theodosius did this to unify the entire empire behind the Orthodox Catholic position. The Catholics also wanted to squash the Arians. In fact, the Arians and the Catholics were still quarreling through their various councils, which only neutralized one another without materially advancing their doctrinal views. So with the emperor's help, the Catholics wanted to secure their victory.

At the council, 150 bishops were there in attendance. Meletius, Gregory of Nazianzus, and Nectarius of Constantinople worked together and presided over the council. According to Christian scholar D. S. Scrum, the following occurred at this council:

> The council condemned the Pneumatomachian heresy (which denied the divinity of the Holy Spirit), the Sabellians, Eunomians, Apollinarians, and virtually completed the orthodox dogma of the Holy Trinity.

In other words, the council ratified the Nicene Creed in order to make it sound more Trinitarian in language and theology. Also, this council settled the great issue of the relation of the Holy Spirit to God. According to David K. Bernard, many Catholics thought that the Holy Ghost was a creature, an angelic being, or an energy. But the council added statements to the original Nicene Creed to teach that the Holy

Spirit is a separate person like God the Father and God the Son. So this was the first council to state that the Father, Son, and Holy Spirit are three separate persons of God. The Catholic Church will now teach that the three persons of God are coequal, coeternal, and of co-essence. This is false doctrine!

Theodosius had to deal with the Goths that were ravaging the east. So in AD 382, he, through half-Roman half- barbarian General Stilicho (AD 365–408), made a deal with the Visigoths. He promised them land in the empire as long as they fight as soldiers in the Roman army. In fact, Theodosius made a treaty with them. But this treaty ended in AD 394. This is when Theodosius led his Roman troops to the Battle of Frigidus. This battle occurred because a man named Arbogast murdered the Western Emperor Valentinian II (AD 375–392) in order to be the ruler of the west. Alaric (AD 370–410) and his Gothic troops accompanied Theodosius and his army.

At the Battle of Frigidus, the emperor deliberately chose to put Alaric's army on the frontline. This battle was brutal, but Theodosius defeated Arbogast and his army. This victory made Theodosius the sole ruler of the Roman Empire. But this victory was bitter sweet for Alaric, who lost ten thousand of his men on the battlefield. Alaric was devastated by the deaths of his men. He cared about his people. Never again will he allow his people to be mere casualties for the Romans. So from this time forward, Alaric and the Visigoths, as well as other barbarian tribes, will be a greater and constant threat to the Roman Empire. (This is especially true in the fifth century.) In the following year, Theodosius died of natural causes. After his death, the Roman Empire was permanently divided into the western empire and eastern empire.

Now besides Athanasius, the Catholic Church had their champions of the Trinitarian doctrine. These men are Cyril of Jerusalem (AD 313–386), Hilary of Poitiers (AD 300–368), Basil (AD 330–379), Ambrose of Milan (AD 339–397), John Chrysostom (AD 345–407),

Gregory of Nazianzus (AD 329–389), Jerome (AD 347–420), Pope Damasus I (AD 305–384), and Gregory of Nyssa (AD 335–395). All of these men preached the Nicene Creed, and they defended the Catholic mode and formula of baptism. The writings of these men prove this fact. Also, history records that the preachers of Arianism were the biggest opponents of these Catholic fathers. But the fathers also had problems with God's ekklesia. And the problem was this: The water baptism into the name of Jesus. Scholar W. H. T. Dau wrote the following:

> The baptisms recorded in the NT after Pentecost are administered "in the name of Jesus Christ" (Acts 2:38), "in the name of the Lord Jesus" (8:16), "into Christ" (Rom. 6:3; Gal. 3:27). This difficulty was considered by the fathers. Ambrose says: "What had not been mentioned in words is expressed in belief." (*De Spiritu Sancto* i.3.43)

In other words, the Catholic Church continued to baptize souls in the name of the Father, Son, and Holy Spirit because that's what they believe. But their belief is due to the blindness of their minds because there's no Holy Scripture to use to support their baptism. So instead of humbling themselves, they decided to continue to do things their way. They are without excuse. Once again, if you suppress the truth and righteousness of God, God's truth and righteousness becomes more obvious. These men defended the Nicene Creed till their deaths.

During this period, something changed within the Catholic Church. The change was this: Catholics were no longer receiving the gift of the Holy Ghost with the evidence of speaking in tongues. This happened because the Roman Catholic Church went so far away from God in their theology. False doctrine is sin. The apostle Peter said this in Acts 5:32, "And we are His witnesses of these things; and so is also the Holy Ghost, whom God has given to them that obey Him." So the Lord Yeshua stopped pouring out the Holy Spirit on the Catholics because of their persistence in disobeying His commandments. Speaking in tongues as the Spirit of God gives utterance had practically disappeared in the Catholic Church.

John Chrysostom recognized that this was happening. He remembered the fact that Catholics used to speak in other languages after receiving the Holy Spirit. He wrote the following:

> This whole place is very obscure: but the obscurity is produced by our ignorance of the facts referred to and by their cessation, being such as then used to occur but now no longer take place...Well: what did happen then? Whoever was baptized he straightway spoke with tongues...they at once on their baptism received the Spirit...[They] began to speak, one in the tongue of the Persians, another in that of the Romans, another in that of the Indians, or in some other language. And this disclosed to outsiders that it was the Spirit in the speaker.

If you do not do what God says after hearing the truth of God's word and repent, then you will never receive the Spirit of Christ. And if any man or woman does not have the Spirit of Christ, then you are not a saint of God. Your soul is in danger while you are reading this book. I say this because I love you.

Almost every Christian scholar on earth will tell you that the Old and New Testament does not teach the doctrine of the Trinity. In fact, Catholic scholar R. L. Richard wrote the following in the *New Catholic Encyclopedia*:

> When one does speak of an unqualified Trinitarianism, one has moved from the period of Christian ori-gins to, say, the last quadrant of the 4th century. It was only then that what might be called the defini-tive Trinitarian dogma "one God in three Persons" became thoroughly assimilated into Christian life and thought.

Mr. Richard also wrote,

> On the other hand, the formula itself does not reflect the immediate consciousness of the period of origins; it was the product of 3 centuries of doctrinal development.

So it took three centuries for the Catholic Church to develop the doctrine of the Trinity. Even the Catholic Church knows the truth. This is what happens when the traditions of men supplants the knowledge and will of God. The truth about God is in the Holy Bible alone. But the Catholics couldn't understand it because they refused to put off the ways of the world and repent. So they had to come up with their own doctrine to explain their beliefs. This is unacceptable to the Lord Jesus. God is not pleased!

Now the Catholic Church still had problems evangelizing souls. This was the case before and after the Council of Constantinople. Even though the Catholics were increasing in number throughout the fourth century, it was hard for them to convince people that the Trinity is a reality. Why? It is not taught in the Holy Scriptures. So the Catholic Church did something to try to solve this problem. This is what they did: They expanded the text of 1 John 5:7. Scholar Massey H. Shepherd, Jr. wrote the following:

> During the controversies of the 4th cent. over the doctrine of the Trinity the text was expanded—first in Spain *ca.* 380, and then taken up in the Vulg.—by the insertion: "There are three that bear record in heaven, the Father, the Word, and the Holy Spirit: and these three are one." A few late Greek manuscripts contain the addition. Hence it passed into the kjv. But all modern critical editions and translations of the NT, including the rsv, omit the interpolation, as it has no warrant in the best and most ancient manuscripts or in the early church fathers.

I tell the truth. I lie not. The first part of 1 John 5:7 in the kjv is an interpolation (altering by putting in new words without authorization). In other words, the Catholic Church did this without God's authorization! Now am I saying that you should throw away your King James Bible? Of course not! There's power in the kjv. Besides, what the devil meant for evil, God meant for good. Let me explain.

The King James Version of 1 John 5:7 says that the Father, the Word (Logos), and the Holy Ghost are one. This is the truth. David A. Huston wrote the following in his online article:

> The word logos can have two meanings which are different yet closely related. It can mean a thought or idea, but it can also mean the __expression of a thought or idea. The Greeks used the term "interior logos," which means an idea, a concept, or a mental image. They also used the term "exterior logos," which refers to the __expression or actualization of an idea or concept.

David A. Huston continues to make his point by saying,

> In the Bible, the Logos was God's plan. In the beginning was the Plan, and the Plan was with God [in His mind], and the Plan was God [that He would make Himself known].

Before Christ came in the flesh, He existed in the mind of God as the interior Logos. But when the Logos was made flesh, God's plan of salvation came to fruition as the exterior Logos. Now let us consider what the Holy Scriptures teach us. Elohim (God) is a Spirit (John 4:24). He is one huge Spirit that is everywhere and fills everything, including the universe and heaven itself. In fact, King Solomon said that heaven itself cannot contain God (1 Kings 8:27). God's Spirit dwells above the highest heaven; this is why He is called the Most High God. And this Spirit is holy by nature. So this Spirit is called the Holy Ghost. (Ghost is an Old-English word for spirit.) The Holy Spirit created everything in the beginning (Gen. 1), and He is still creating people and things. This is why the Holy Spirit is God the Father. This same Spirit caused the conception of the Son in Mary's womb. This is more proof that the Holy Ghost is God the Father (Matt. 1:20). And from the moment of conception to His birth, the Son of God is God made known in the flesh. The Son is the Logos (Word) made flesh; He is God and man fused together.

The Logos was sent into the world to be our savior by suffering and dying for our sins. And after God the Father raised the Son from the dead, He sat the Messiah on the throne of the right hand of God. Jesus Christ was the Word of God before glorification while He was on earth. But now He is the Word after glorification. So there are three that bear record in heaven, the Father, the Word, and the Holy Ghost: and these three aspects of the One true God are one. This is why the Catholic Church never agreed with the theology of the original and primitive ekklesia. The ekklesia and the Jews believe that God is one. And according to these groups, the word *one*, as it is used to describe God, means one, not united. So by trying to insert a Trinitarian passage into the Scripture, they did more to prove the fact that God is one. Keep your kjv Bible saints! As for the rest of you, be ye saved, read your kjv Bible (or other version) and ask God to give you His understanding of what thus saith His most precious and sacred Holy Word!

Prior to the fifth century, the Scriptures of the Holy Bible were finally canonized by the Roman Catholic Church. This process started in the second century and was finished toward the end of this century. During this period, the ekklesia, as a whole, did not have any major problems recognizing the books of the Old Testament (whether from the Hebrew Tanakh or Greek Septuagint) and of the New Testament. But as for the Catholic Church, the process of canonizing the Scriptures into a list of God-breathed books was done by trial and error. In fact, the Catholic Church used the books of the Apocrypha in addition to the Holy Scriptures. Scholar Lou H. Silberman wrote the following:

> Cyril of Jerusalem in his catechism of 348 indicated the canon of the OT to be the Jewish Scriptures in the order found in the LXX with the addition of Baruch and the Letter of Jeremiah. In Palestine, as in Egypt, other books were permitted public reading, though the scope of such permitted works varied. It included in various combinations II, III Macc., Wisd. Sol., Pss. and Odes of Solomon, Ecclus., Esth., Judith, Tobit, and Susanna.

So the books of the Apocrypha have been a part of the Catholic Church's Bible for a long time. Why? This is because of the Septuagint (LXX). It consisted of the Greek Old Testament and the books of the Apocrypha. But the Hebrew Tanakh never did include the books of the Apocrypha.

When the Jews translated the Hebrew Bible into Greek during the so-called silent years, the LXX did include the books of the Apocrypha. But the Jews only used those books for historical references and for some religious purposes. The Jews never considered the Apocryphal books to be inspired by Elohim. Lou H. Silberman also wrote,

> It was this enlarged collection that was accepted by the African churches at the synods of Hippo (393) and Carthage (397) and from there traveled to Rome, where it was accepted over the cents.

Let me make myself clear: The books of the Apocrypha were not God-breathed! These books do not testify of Jesus the Messiah, and they teach damnable doctrines that are contrary to all Scripture (i.e., a person committing suicide while still being righteous). Also, the Catholic Church changed the order of the books of the Tanakh to the gentile canon that is now called the Old Testament. Based on my research, this was partially done because of the order of the books that make up the Septuagint. If there are other reasons for this change, they are not known. All we can do is speculate. Lastly, the Synod of

Carthage also issued the list of the books of the New Testament that is the same as today.

While all these things were happening within the empire, God's messianic community continued to win souls throughout the known world. But the ekklesia suffered some hardships as well. For example, the Catholics of Constantinople confiscated the Cappadocian Apostolic churches in AD 361. And in AD 390, Emperor Theodosius killed 7,000 saints at Thessalonica. Nevertheless, God's ekklesia continued to baptize sinners in the name of the Lord Jesus, and God Himself filled these sinners with the precious gift of the Holy Ghost. And because of this, speaking in other tongues (which was called *glossolalia*) continued within the messianic community. With the Lord Yeshua on their side, the saints of God marched triumphantly into the fifth century.

THE FIFTH CENTURY

A lot of things changed within the Roman Empire. Roman Catholicism is the official religion of the empire, and the Catholic Church is a powerful religious organization. Greek is no longer the common language of the empire. It was replaced with Latin. (This shift occurred in the fourth century.) The Catholic Church did have a Latin version of the New Testament called the *Vetus Latina*. There were even Latin versions of the Old Testament that were translated from the LXX. But in AD 382, Jerome, a Catholic father, began his work of making a better Latin version of the Old and New Testament.

First, he translated the New Testament Scriptures into Latin by correcting the *Vetus Latina*. Then in AD 390, Jerome began his work of translating the Hebrew Tanakh into Latin. He completed his Latin Vulgate in AD 405. But unfortunately, the Apocrypha (in the Latin language) was also included in Jerome's Latin version of the Bible.

The Roman Empire itself was in peril. Like I said in the previous chapter, the Roman Empire had to recruit the barbarians into their army and depend on them to help the empire defend itself. But the Romans treated them harshly. So because of the Roman's prejudice and harsh treatment of the barbarians, the barbarians turned against the weakened empire. And to make things worst, the Huns invaded the tribal villages at the margins of the empire in the west. The Huns destroyed everything in their path, including the already dwindling Roman army. The Huns took no prisoners and left no survivors. Italy itself was in complete danger of being taken over by the barbarians.

In AD 406, the Roman army in Italy was in desperate need of soldiers. In order to recruit soldiers, General Stilicho traveled to the Gothic King Alaric's camp located in Illyricum to make a deal with him. Alaric had the right number of men behind him needed to help Stilicho defend Northern Italy. The Gothic King wanted a Treaty with Rome; he never wanted to take over the empire. Stilicho promised Alaric a Roman command. Also, Stilicho promised Alaric that his men will be well-paid by the Western Emperor Honorius (AD 393–423) as long as the Goths help him recapture Illyricum. So in the next two years Alaric delivers his end of the bargain. But Honorius refuses to pay the Goths for their services. In fact, one of Honorius's advisors turns the emperor against Stilicho. So in AD 408, Honorius issued a decree against Stilicho. The barbarian general fled and sought refuge in a Catholic church in Ravenna. When the Roman army found him, Stilicho willingly gave himself up to his captors. After he was captured, Stilicho was executed in public. Most historians consider this to be a tragedy because Stilicho was one of the last great leaders of the Roman Empire in the fifth century.

Stilicho's death automatically killed the treaty he made with Alaric. Also, the hatred towards the barbarians intensified. According to Noel Lenski, professor at the University of Colorado, the Romans swept through the towns of Italy and massacred ten thousand barbarians. The ones who survived fled to Alaric. Thirty thousand men joined Alaric's army, and Alaric and his men went to Rome, Italy, to pressure Honorius into giving them what they want. Alaric arrived at Rome in AD 410. He had no intentions of conquering the city. All Alaric wants is to meet with the emperor and come to some kind of an agreement.

Honorius sent word to Alaric that he is willing to make a deal with him. So Alaric leaves Rome to meet the emperor in Ravenna. But along the way, mercenaries that work for the emperor ambushed Alaric and his army. The emperor tried to kill Alaric and cut down his army. They failed! After defeating the Roman mercenaries, Alaric leads his men back to Rome. Alaric is now bent on Rome's destruction.

In AD 410, the Goths broke through the gates of the great city. For the first time in eight hundred years, Rome itself is sacked by an enemy. Like I said, Alaric didn't want to do this. But the empire left him no choice. For three days, the citizens of Rome were killed, and the city was plundered of its riches. According to the History Channel's documentary "Rome: Rise and Fall of an Empire," Jerome wrote about this horrible event in Roman history. He wrote, "The city which had conquered the whole world was itself conquered." After this happened, Emperor Honorius did nothing to help the citizens of Rome. As a result, the people began to lose faith in the emperor's ability to defend and protect them from the empire's foreign invaders. And when Alaric died due to an illness, the Visigoths continued to cut down the empire's dwindling army. So over the next four decades, the Roman Empire in the west lost huge chunks of land to the barbarians. And things only got worse as the Huns continued to go through Roman villages like a tornado. The empire was powerless to stop the various barbarian tribes. This was the beginning of the end of the Roman Empire as we know it.

While all this chaos was happening, the Roman Catholic Church was becoming progressively worse. For example, Pope Innocent I (AD 401–417) claimed that the pope was the universal leader of the Catholic religion. We're all familiar with this old saying, "Power corrupts, and absolute power corrupts absolutely." So what did the Catholic Church do with their power? They persecuted and killed the saints and other so-called Christian groups that they labeled as heretics. For instance, around AD 411, Augustine (AD 354–430) had Emperor Honorius massacre the Donatists in North Africa. According to Marvin M.

Arnold, these Donatists were Pentecostal. So it is very probable that they were members of God's apostolic ekklesia. Besides, the messianic community in Africa still outnumbered the African Catholics. In fact, in AD 402, there were only about sixty-four Catholic bishops in Africa and Asia Minor combined. So while the saints of God prayed for and showed compassion to the Catholics despite their differences, the Catholics hated God's ekklesia because of what they believed. See the difference? Also, on May 1, 418, the Catholic Church reasserted its teaching on infant baptism at the Council of Carthage. The council stated that infants must be baptized so that sin may be remitted. Like I said, the Catholic Church was getting worse.

Now besides the Pope, Augustine was a prominent member of the Catholic Church. He converted to Catholicism and was baptized into the Trinity in AD 387. Augustine was heavily influenced by the philosophies of Neo- Platonism and Plotinus. So he developed his own approach to philosophy and theology, for Augustine believed that Catholicism was the true philosophy. So after the completion of the Nicene Creed, the Catholics were still relying on Greek philosophy to understand the Holy Scriptures. This is why Colossians 2:8 warns us about worldly philosophy, for it is another form of bondage. About ten years after his conversion, Augustine became the bishop of the Catholic Church in ancient Hippo.

Throughout the rest of his life, Augustine dealt with the Manichaean, Donatist, and Pelagian controversies. He even struggled against the Arians in North Africa. Also, he wrote over fifty different books, which contain many of his quotations. Till this day, Augustine is famous for his many theological quotes. For instance, he testified that the Catholic Church in his day did not speak in unknown tongues after receiving the Holy Ghost. But Augustine admitted that this used to be the case. In his work titled "On Baptism, Against the Donatists," Augustine wrote the following:

> For the Holy Spirit is not only given by the laying on of hands amid the testimony of temporal sensible miracles, as He was given in former days... For who expects in these days that those on whom hands are laid that they may receive the Holy Spirit should forthwith begin to speak with tongues?

As I mentioned in the previous chapter, John Chrysostom acknowledged the fact that the Catholic Church was no longer receiving the Holy Ghost with the evidence of speaking in other languages. But Augustine stated that speaking in tongues immediately when receiving the Holy Ghost is not expected at all. This is how bad the Catholic Church was in God's sight during Augustine's day.

Here is another one of Augustine's famous quotes: "Anyone who denies the Trinity is in danger of losing his salvation, and anyone who tries to understand it is in danger of losing his mind." The Trinity is not real, so you don't have to worry about losing your salvation. But the latter part of Augustine's quotation is so true. The doctrine of the Trinity is not a spiritual doctrine. It is of the devil, and this most unclean spirit used unwise men to create this doctrine. The more you try to understand it with your carnal mind, the quicker you go crazy! But as for the saints who are spiritual, the more you try to understand the Trinity, the more you realize that it doesn't make any sense. The Messiah Jesus is the Son of God, which means that He is the One true God revealed in human flesh. When he became old and unwell, Augustine fell asleep as a Catholic due to illness.

Another Catholic creed emerged sometime after Augustine's death. This creed is called the Athanasian Creed. No scholar or Christian historian knows who wrote this creed. In fact, some scholars believe that this creed was written in the late fifth century. Others believe that it was written during the time of Augustine because its Trinitarian theology is very similar to Augustine's theology. This creed was named after Athanasius, who had then been dead for decades. This creed is more

Catholic in its theology than the revised Nicene Creed. For instance, the Athanasian Creed states the following:

So the Father is God, the Son is God, and the Holy Ghost is God. And yet they are not Three Gods, but One God. So likewise the Father is Lord, the Son Lord, and the Holy Ghost Lord. And yet not Three Lords but One Lord.

This makes no sense! If you read the Holy Bible, you will find out that the doctrine of the Trinity is not taught or spoken of at all. This is the truth! With the Nicene and Athanasian Creeds in the Catholic Church's possession, the doctrine of the Trinity is now complete.

There was another false teaching on Christianity that was irritating the Catholic Church: Nestorianism. This doctrine teaches that the divine nature and the human nature of Christ are separate in the man Christ Jesus. In other words, the humanity and divinity of Christ are not one in Him. This false teaching was started by a man named Nestorius (AD 386–451), and he was the archbishop of Constantinople from AD 428–431. Also, Nestorius objected to the use of the term *theotokos*, which means "God-bearer" and "the one who gives birth to God." This term was used by Catholics to refer to Mary as the Mother of God. Nestorius also believed that this title denied Christ's humanity. So he proposed the use of the term *Christotokos*, which means Christ-bearer. Nestorius believed that this term better emphasized the unity of the two natures of Jesus. He was so confused.

The Catholic Church felt that they had to do something about Nestorius's false teachings. So in AD 431, the Catholic Church responded to the doctrines of Nestorius by calling the Council of Ephesus. This is the third Ecumenical Council in the history of Roman Catholicism. Approximately 250 bishops were present at the council. Nestorius and his bishops were there to represent their views, and they were up against the Catholic champion Cyril of Alexandria (AD 376–444). The council itself consisted of seven different sessions, and the Catholics triumphed over Nestorius. Cyril and his fellow bishops were able to win the victory for the Catholic religion. They condemned Nestorius and his teachings. Then Nestorius was deposed and banished to Egypt. Also, eight canons were passed on various doctrinal matters. Lastly, the council decreed that the Nicene Creed should never be changed but should remain forever as the standard of the Catholic Church's faith. All of these things precipitated the Nestorian Schism. For instance, the churches that were supportive of Nestorius, especially in Persia, were severed from the Roman Catholic Church. They became known as the Nestorian Church or the Church of the East. So the council ended with unresolved issues between the Catholics and the Nestorians.

Sometime later, an archmonk named Eutyches (AD 380–456) was deposed by Patriarch Flavian of Constantinople on account of his Christological point of view. Eutyches believed that Christ has only one nature, in which His divinity and humanity are literally one. This is not biblical. The Holy Bible teaches us that the dual nature of the Messiah consists of his manly human nature and His divine nature that have been fused together. So the two different natures of the Messiah are one. The Christology of Eutyches is an early version of what later became known as Monophysitism. Dioscurus, the Patriarch of Alexandria, supported Eutyches and saw this action as an injustice. So in AD 449, Dioscurus influenced Emperor Theodosius II (AD 408–450) to call the Second Council of Ephesus to deal with the matter.

A total number of 198 bishops were present at the council, and Dioscurus of Alexandria presided over the council. They discussed the issue of whether Flavian had acted properly in deposing and excommunicating Eutyches. After much discussion, it was decided that Flavian did not act properly in deposing Eutyches. He was cleared of guilt of his Christology, and Eutyches was reinstated to his position. Then Dioscurus led the bishops in deposing Flavian from his post. There were 135 bishops who ultimately joined in signing the canon removing him. Some other things did happen at the council, but they are insignificant. Now the drama is about to begin.

What is significant is the power that Dioscurus tried to exercise during and after the council. The online *Catholic Encyclopedia* states the following about Dioscurus:

> He went to Constantinople and appointed his secretary Anatolius bishop of that great see. Juvenal of Jerusalem had become his tool, he had deposed the Patriarchs of Antioch and Constantinople; but one powerful adversary yet remained. He halted at Nicaea, and with ten bishops (no doubt the ten Egyptian metropolitans whom he had brought to Ephesus), 'in addition to all his other crimes he extended his madness against him who had been entrusted with the guardianship of the Vine by the Saviour'—in the words of the bishops at Chalcedon—and excommunicated the pope himself.

As a result of Dioscurus's actions, Pope Leo I (AD 440–461) responded by excommunicating him and everyone else who had taken part in the council. Also, Leo I absolved all whom the council had condemned except Domnus of Antioch, who chose to retire. He even declared all the actions of the council to be null and void. But because of the Second Council of Ephesus, the tide had turned away from Nestorianism and toward the condemnation of Monophysitism. This will lead to another ecumenical council.

In order to assert the Orthodox Catholic teaching against the heresies of Eutyches and the Monophysites, the Eastern Emperor Marcian (AD 450–457) convoked the Council of Chalcedon in AD 451. This council was also called because Pope Leo I wanted to right the wrongs committed at the Second Council of Ephesus. But Leo was not present at the council; he sent his own legates to represent him. This council lasted for sixteen sessions, and it was presided by a board of government officials and senators led by the patrician Anatolius. Six hundred bishops participate in this ecumenical council. And most of these bishops came from the east.

In the first session, the members of the council read the Acts of the Robber Council (Second Council of Ephesus) along with those of the synod held in AD 448 by Flavian of Constantinople. After this happened, the imperial commissioners declared that Dioscurus and the leaders in the Robber Council should suffer the same punishment that Flavian and the other bishops had suffered by that synod. Towards the end of the first session, all declared themselves satisfied with the deposition of Dioscurus alone.

In the second session, the following was read aloud at the council: The creeds of the Councils of Nicaea and of Constantinople; two letters of Cyril of Alexandria, Cyril's second letter to Nestorius and the letter written to the Antiochene bishops in AD 433 after his reconciliation with them; and finally the dogmatic epistle of Pope Leo I. All these documents were approved by the council. This makes perfect sense because all of these documents contain the doctrines of the Roman Catholic Church.

In the third session, new accusations were brought against Dioscurus. Catholic scholar Francis Schaefer wrote the following:

> Eusebius of Dorylaeum presented a new accusation against Dioscurus of Alexandria in which the charges of heresy and of injustice committed in the Robber Council of Ephesus were repeated. Three ecclesiastics and a layman from Alexandria likewise presented accusations against their bishop; he was declared guilty of many acts of injustice and of personal misconduct. At the end of the session the papal legates declared that Dioscurus should be deprived of his bishopric and of all ecclesiastical dignities for having supported the heretic Eutyches, for having excommunicated Pope Leo, and for having refused to answer the charges made against him.

Wow! Talk about a courtroom drama! All the members present agreed to this proposition. The council decreed to depose Dioscurus, and the decree of deposition was communicated to him. Also, the decree was communicated to the Alexandrine ecclesiastics with him at Chalcedon, to Emperors Marcian and Valentinian III (AD 425–455) and to the Empress Pulcheria.

The fourth session comprised two meetings that was held on October 17 and 20. During these meetings, the epistle of Pope Leo was approved once again by the bishops who were present. Also, Juvenal of Jerusalem, Thalassius of Caesarea in Cappadocia, Eusebius of Ancyra, Eustathius of Berytus, Basil of Seleucia in Cicilia, and former partisans of Dioscurus in the Second Council of Ephesus were pardoned and admitted to the sessions. Then the council decided to investigate the orthodoxy of a number of bishops from Egypt, and of a number of monks and archimandrites suspected of teaching the doctrines of Eutychianism.

In the fifth session, the bishops published a decree concerning the Catholic faith. This decree is considered to be the specific dogmatic decree of the Fourth General Council. The decrees of the Councils of Nicaea, Constantinople, and the First Council of Ephesus, as well as the teaching of Cyril against Nestorius and the dogmatic epistle of Pope Leo were again approved by the members of the council. They used these decrees and epistles to produce a decree that states the following:

> We teach…one and the same Christ, Son, Lord, Only-begotten, known in two natures, without confusion, without change, without division, without separation.

The Holy Bible already teaches this great truth about Jesus the Messiah. After reciting this decree to the council all the bishops exclaimed that such was the true faith. They agreed that all should at once sign their names to it. Then the imperial commissioners announced that they would communicate to the emperor the decree as approved by all the bishops. This was the most important session of this council.

In the sixth session, the emperor himself was present. The decree of the Catholic faith that was made in the preceding session was read again and approved by the emperor. The members of the council that were present made joyful acclamations to the emperor and to the empress, in which they were compared to Constantine and Helena. After this happened, the session ended.

The final goal of the council was achieved in the sixth session. So in the remaining sessions, only secondary matters were transacted. They were not significant at all. But I do want to talk about the fifteenth session because it produced and approved twenty-eight disciplinary canons. I will talk about just two: the fifteenth and sixteenth canons. The fifteenth canon stated that once a woman was ordained a deaconess, she couldn't leave her state of residence and marry. And the sixteenth canon stated that virgins and monks consecrated to God could not get married at all. Forbidding marriage is exactly what 1 Timothy 4:3 talks about. And this is just one of the many New Testament prophecies that apply to the Roman Catholic Church. But at that time, certain clerics, including the pope, were still allowed to get married. (The Roman Catholic Church did not officially forbid marriage to all clerics, including the pope, until the twelfth century.) Like I said, the Holy Bible clearly states that you will know the difference between those who belong to God and those who don't by their fruits.

As a result of the Council of Chalcedon, Eutyches and Dioscurus were both banished. But the council didn't end the controversy concerning the two natures of Christ. Catholic scholar Francis Schaefer wrote the following:

> The Council of Chalcedon…did not put an end to the controversy concerning the natures of Christ and their relation to each other. Many people in the East disliked the term *person* used by the council to signify the union of, or the means of uniting, the two natures in Christ. They believed that Nestorianism was thereby renewed; or at

least they thought the definition less satisfactory than St. Cyril's concept of the union of the two natures in Christ. (Bardenhewer, *Patrologie*, second ed., 321–322)

So Nestorianism, Eutychianism, and Monophysitism continued to prevail long after the council ended. The monks and ecclesiastics in Palestine, Syria, Armenia, Egypt, and other countries refused to accept the definition of the council. In fact, the Monophysites are found there to this day.

While the Roman Empire was crumbling from within in the first half of the fifth century, Elohim was adding souls to the ekklesia daily. For instance, when the barbarians and Vandals were invading the Roman Empire in waves the average Roman citizen was fearful for their lives. But the saints were not afraid of the barbarian invasions. In fact, many barbarians and Vandals came in contact with God's ekklesia while they were ravaging the western empire. But Yeshua gave His saints favor with them, and some of the barbarians were born again of the water and of the Spirit.

During this period, the Catholics were persecuting the ekklesia. In fact, they were persecuting God's elect so badly that the saints sought protection under the Goths and Vandals. And many of these barbarians were Arians in their theology. In addition, there was a city in ancient France called Toulouse. This city was not only a Gothic state, it was protected as an apostolic (or sanctified) stronghold as early as AD 419. Also, the seven churches that are mentioned in Revelation 1–3 were still alive and well. They were still preaching the gospel of Jesus according to the Scriptures and teaching the apostle's doctrine.

The messianic community was also winning over the rejects of the Catholic Church. For instance, many Nestorians were converted and became saints during the thirties and forties of this century. The gift of the Holy Ghost was being poured out on many sinners in Western Europe, especially Frisia, Saxony, and Languedoc. Also, God was pouring out His Spirit on sinners who were Montanists, Manichee,

Samosatenes, and Artemonites. These people were also baptized in the name of Jesus the Messiah. In addition, the churches were increasing in number and spreading further into Africa. And Jesus was gushing His Spirit on much of the eastern hemisphere, especially Persia and China. The gates of hell were not prevailing against God's ekklesia, and Yeshua was fulfilling His word by not leaving Himself without tongue-talking witnesses in the ancient world.

By the time the Council of Chalcedon ended, the Roman Empire had lost huge chunks of land in the west. Most of North Africa was conquered by the barbarians, including much land in ancient Great Britain and Portugal. The Huns, led by Attila (AD 434–453), captured a lot of land as well. The Huns would've caused more damage to the empire if Attila had lived. He died suddenly of a broken blood vessel on his wedding night. His new bride was so scared of being accused of killing him that she spent the entire night with Attila's dead body. She saved her life by doing this. Attila's death caused the immediate collapse of the mighty Huns. But the demise of the Huns didn't save the western empire.

In AD 455, the ancient city of Rome is sacked again by Vandal barbarians from North Africa. According to Thomas R. Martin, professor at the College of the Holy Cross, the Romans were shocked and terrified that the barbarians could come to Rome and literally take whatever they want. For two weeks, the Vandals plundered and looted great amounts of treasure from the city. And during the fifties of this century, the empire lost control of the Mediterranean because of centuries of endless waves of barbarian attacks. Desperate, the empire negotiated with them and gave the barbarians some of its most fertile land. The empire simply gave away all of ancient Great Britain, Spain, and small parts of Gaul. The eastern empire remained strong, but the west was getting weaker by the year. Also, the Roman army was a shell of itself. The supreme fighting skills, discipline, and tactics of the army are now gone. In fact, the Roman army has been a shell of itself for decades.

The Roman army is now almost entirely of barbarian decent. But old ethnic tensions were dividing the army. Within the army itself, the Romans were fighting against the barbarians. But in AD 456, General Flavius Ricimer (AD 405–472) came on the scene. He was of Germanic decent, and he was an Arian. Ricimer was determined to maintain order in the Roman army and gain more power in the western empire. So Ricimer gathered his troops and marched to Agrigentum (located in modern-day Sicily) to fight the Vandals of Carthage. This was a bloody and brutal battle. But despite the great onslaught of barbarians, Ricimer and his army defeated them. This was a great victory for Ricimer. But he is not the only one who is trying to ascend to the throne of the western empire. He is up against two of his old friends in the Roman army: Majorian and Aegidius. Ricimer was also up against the western emperor Avitus (AD 455–456).

Now Avitus was a terrible emperor. He neglected his imperial duties and enjoyed the luxuries of being emperor of the west. This was during a period when famine had gripped the provinces of the west. This happened because the Vandals had seized the west's food supply, which came from North Africa. The poor had two choices: steal food for survival or starve to death. Avitus was not popular at all in Italy. In fact, he was so unpopular that the people were rioting in the streets of Rome. Avitus was literally chased out of Rome. So he fled Italy and traveled to Gaul to gather Gothic supporters in order to reclaim his throne.

Ricimer and Majorian saw their opportunity to seize power in the west. While Avitus and his Gothic troops were on their way back to Italy, Ricimer and Majorian, along with the Roman army, ambushed them. After a brutal battle, Ricimer and Majorian defeats the Goths and capture Avitus on the battlefield. Then Ricimer spares his life and deposes him. In the same year, Avitus was made a bishop of a Catholic church in the same Italian city where he was deposed. Then Ricimer secretly sends his friend Majorian to assassinate Avitus. Majorian murdered the deposed emperor and Catholic bishop.

In the following year, Ricimer made Majorian (AD 457–461) the emperor of the west. Ricimer wanted to be emperor, but he knew that he wouldn't be tolerated because of his barbarian roots. So Ricimer made Majorian the emperor because he thought that he could control his appointed emperor. He wanted Majorian to be his puppet on the throne.

Majorian made Ricimer the master of soldiers in Italy, and he sent Aegidius to Gaul to defend it against the various barbarian tribes that were constantly invading it. Majorian was no puppet. In fact, Majorian was indeed a competent emperor. He recognized the deficiencies of the western empire and tried to rectify them. He wanted to restore the west more than anybody. So Majorian devised a grand military campaign against the Vandal king Gaiseric (AD 389–477) to recapture North Africa. Ricimer was not pleased.

In AD 461, Majorian led his troops to Hispania. His plan was to build very efficient ships and then use them to overpower the Vandals of North Africa. He needed to do this in order to restore the west's food supply and revenue. But on a dreadful night, Vandals secretly invade Majorian's camp and set all his ships on fire. Once again, the Vandals proved to be too much for the empire. Majorian's military campaign was over. This was a crushing defeat for the western empire. So Majorian went back to Italy. While the emperor was traveling back to Rome, Ricimer and his band of soldiers intercepted Majorian. They arrested the emperor, stripped him of his crown, and chopped his head off. Ricimer did this because he realized that he couldn't control Majorian.

When Aegidius heard the news of Majorian's death, he broke away from Ricimer and refused to acknowledge his power. Ricimer saw this as an act of war against him. So he prepared for war against Aegidius. While he was doing this, Ricimer chose a man who he thought would be a much better puppet for him to control. His name is Libius Severus (AD 461–465). Ricimer's plan was to crush Aegidius on the battlefield through his puppet emperor. On the other hand, Aegidius was determined to defend his so-called kingdom in Soissons against Ricimer at all costs.

Aegidius and his army in Gaul are ready to fight against Ricimer and his army. His plan was to invade Italy and fight Ricimer and his army there. But Ricimer knew about this. He had to act quickly to block Aegidius's impending attack. So in AD 463, Ricimer, through Emperor Severus, makes a deal with the empire's one time enemy: the Visigoths. Once his alliance with the Visigoths was complete, Ricimer hires them to attack Aegidius while he was on his way to Italy. The Goths met Aegidius and his army on the battlefield outside the city of Orleans. This was another brutal battle. But Aegidius knew that he was fighting for the survival of the empire. So he and his army did what they could to chop the barbarians down. After a brutal and bloody battle, Aegidius emerged victorious on the battlefield. But his army suffered heavy losses. And he knew that his army would not survive another wave of barbarian attacks.

Desperate, Aegidius sent a messenger to Gaiseric, the Vandal king, to make a deal with him. If the news of this action would've gotten out, Aegidius would've become very unpopular. After all, Gaiseric had captured North Africa and cut off the western empire's food supply during the forties of this century. But he had no other options. It is probable that the messenger reached Gaiseric in Africa, but we don't know for sure if an agreement was reached. I say this because Ricimer sent a Roman soldier to assassinate Aegidius while he was waiting for Gaiseric's response. Aegidius was strangled to death in AD 464. Once Aegidius was out of the way, Ricimer's hunger for power increased dramatically. So in the following year, Ricimer had his puppet emperor assassinated as well. He did this because Libius Severus didn't want to remain a puppet. So after the emperor's death, Ricimer ruled the west for eighteen months until eastern emperor Leo I (AD 457–474) named Procopius Anthemius (AD 467–472) as Severus's successor.

While Ricimer ruled the west, Vandals from Africa continued to invade Italy in destructive waves. As the Vandals ravage Italy, they take land away from the western empire piece by piece. While this was happening, Ricimer sat on his throne and did nothing. He literally forced Emperor Leo I to do something to save the western empire. Emperor Leo acted by sending Anthemius and his family to Rome from Constantinople. So in AD 467, Anthemius met Ricimer in Rome. He offered his young and beautiful daughter Alypia in marriage to Ricimer in exchange for the throne. Ricimer welcomed him and married his daughter. He did this because he thought that Anthemius would be another puppet for him while he rules from behind the scenes. But Ricimer will soon find out that he was wrong.

In AD 468, Emperor Leo financed a very large military expedition against the Vandals in Sicily. With the support of the eastern empire, Anthemius led his army to Sicily to fight against the Vandals. When Anthemius reached Sicily, he ordered his men to charge at the barbarians. Ricimer accompanied the western emperor and fought with his army on the battlefield. But Ricimer was not happy at all because his power in the west had diminished significantly. He was so jealous of Anthemius. So due to his jealousy, Ricimer killed his own military commanders. Ricimer did this on the battlefield! In the heat of the battle, he betrayed the empire by deliberately doing his part to sabotage the military campaign! And according to Richard Burgess, professor at the University of Ottawa, the fleet that was headed by Basiliscus, Emperor Leo's brother-in-law, fell apart as well. So Ricimer's actions, as well as other forces, caused the entire military campaign against the Vandals to be a complete disaster. Once again, the Roman Empire in the west suffered another crushing defeat by the barbarians.

After this happened, Anthemius tried to recapture Gaul, which was occupied by the Visigoths. The western emperor and his army fought against the Visigoths in their territory. Unfortunately, the Roman army was defeated because the Gothic army outnumbered Anthemius's army.

This was another crushing defeat for the western empire. And from this point on, the Roman army will be weaker than ever. And to make things worse, the relationship between Anthemius and Ricimer was deteriorating. Things finally came to a boiling point in AD 472.

Ricimer went to Milan and spent months there gathering troops to launch his attack on Anthemius in Rome. Then Ricimer and his army besieged the great city. After several months of constant chaos, Ricimer effectively deposed Emperor Anthemius. The emperor fled Rome and sought refuge in a Catholic church. But it didn't take long for Ricimer to find him. He killed the deposed emperor inside the sanctuary of that Catholic church. And to make things worse, the barbarians were still ravaging various towns in Italy. Also, Ricimer left the city of Rome in complete and utter anarchy. He will forever be remembered as one of the main agents who helped the western empire destroy itself from within. Ricimer ruled in Rome through his new puppet Emperor Anicius Olybrius (AD July 472–November 472) throughout the rest of his days. Then in the same year, he fell asleep as an Arian. Nobody knows exactly how Ricimer died.

In AD 473, Gundobad (AD 452–516), Ricimer's nephew, became the king of another barbarian tribe called the Burgundians. By this period, the Burgundians were living in Gaul. Gundobad is now the head of the western Roman army. And in the same year, Gundobad chose a man named Glycerius (AD 473–474) to be the new emperor of the west. Also, Gundobad made a German soldier named Odovacer (AD 433–493) in charge of his army. In addition, the Roman army is almost entirely made of barbarians. But ethnic tensions still existed between the Roman soldiers that were left in the army and their barbarian counterparts. As a result, violence would occur within the so-called Roman army. There was no unity in the army. And things only got worse as the western empire continued to suffer greater loses against the Visigoths in Gaul.

Since the western empire was no longer able to keep the barbarians from sacking the Mediterranean coastline, eastern emperor Leo tried to solve this problem by appointing Julius Nepos (AD 474–475) as the new emperor of the west. So in AD 474, Nepos led his army from Constantinople to Rome. At first, Glycerius tried to assemble an army to counter Nepos's attack. But Gundobad, the one who appointed Glycerius to be emperor, abandoned him in the time of need. Gundobad went back to his Burgundian Territory and reigned as king. As a result, Glycerius did not have an army that was large enough to fight against Nepos. So as Nepos got closer to Rome, Glycerius met him and surrendered without a fight. Then Nepos spared Glycerius's life, deposed him, and ordered that he be made a Catholic bishop in Dalmatia. Glycerius spent the rest of his life in exile as the Catholic bishop of Salona.

The first thing Emperor Nepos did was promote Roman General Orestes and Odovacer. They were promoted to the highest positions of power in Rome under the emperor. By doing this, Nepos officially sealed the fate of his demise because both men were strong-willed and wanted more power. In fact, Orestes wanted more power than both the emperor and Odovacer combined. Also, Orestes believed that he was the best man for the job of restoring Rome to its glory days. So he was never loyal to Emperor Nepos.

The last Roman province that the west had was Southern Gaul. But it was constantly being raided by the Visigoths led by their king Euric (AD 440–484) . Under Euric's leadership, the Goths have been taking Gaul away from the west piece by piece throughout the seventies of this century. And during Nepos's reign, the Roman army that was stationed at Southern Gaul was forced to battle the Goths. They were no match for them. So Nepos sent Orestes and his army to Gaul to drive out the Goths. This was a big mistake! Instead of fighting against the Goths, Orestes devised a strategy to overthrow Nepos and sideline Odovacer. For instance, Orestes told his mostly barbarian army that if they help him depose Nepos, he will give them valuable land in Italy. The army accepted his offer. So in AD 475, Orestes abandoned Gaul to the Visigoths and went back to Italy to depose Emperor Nepos. As a result, Gaul no longer belonged to Rome and was in the hands of the Visigoths.

Orestes took control of the government at Ravenna and forced Emperor Nepos to flee by ship to Dalmatia. Afterward, Nepos spent the rest of his life in exile. Surprisingly, Orestes did not make himself emperor of the west. Instead, he elevated his son Romulus Augustus (AD 475–476) to the throne. He was twelve years old. Even though Augustus is the new emperor of Rome, his father Orestes ruled from behind the scenes. And Odovacer was no longer a major player in what was left of the western empire.

Sometime later, the barbarians demand Orestes to give them what he had promised. But Orestes refused to give them Italian land. As a result, the barbarians turned to Odovacer for help. They make him an offer he can't refuse. According to scholar Richard Burgess, the barbarians tell Odovacer that they will make him king and ruler over them if he can get them Italian land. Obviously, Odovacer accepts their grand offer.

In AD 476, Odovacer and his barbarian troops raid the cities of Italy. They plunder and destroy everything in their path. Odovacer was bent on usurping his dominance over Italy and Orestes. While the barbarians were closing in on him, Orestes leaves his son in the protective care of his uncle in Ravenna. Then he escapes to Ticinium and seeks refuge in a Catholic church. But it doesn't take Odovacer long to find the church where Orestes was hiding. They plunder the church and burn it to the ground. Fortunately, Orestes managed to escape shortly before his enemies' arrival.

When Odovacer caught up with Orestes near the city of Placentia, the final battle between these two began. This was another brutal battle. Soldiers were climbing over dead bodies as the battle intensified. Orestes was fighting to save the western empire. He refused to accept defeat. But the empire could not be saved. The barbarians were too much for Orestes and his army. So at the battle's end, Orestes and his men were killed with the sword on the battlefield.

After he emerged victorious outside of Placentia, Odovacer went to Ravenna to confront Emperor Augustus. The barbarians came to the residence of the western emperor and killed everyone that stood in their way. Then Odovacer found the terrified young emperor and spared his life. He did this because Augustus was just a puppet on the throne. So at the age of twelve, Augustus was exiled to Castellum Lucullanum in Campania. He is the last Roman emperor of the west. No historian knows exactly what happened to Augustus afterward. He just simply disappeared from the historical record.

Odovacer is now the barbarian king and ruler of Italy. The west is dead. When eastern emperor Zeno (AD 474–475 and 476–491) received the news of what happened to Romulus Augustus, he was devastated. The eastern empire continued to thrive and prosper till the next century. But the empire that was started by Gaius Julius Caesar Augustus in Bc 27 was gone forever. According to scholar Thomas R. Martin, the Roman Empire became strong in the beginning because it encouraged immigration. The outsiders were a huge part of the successful conception of the empire. But centuries later, the Roman Empire became prideful. The Romans thought that they were superior human beings, and everyone else was beneath them. So when the barbarians wanted to become part of the empire, Rome opposed them.

The Roman Empire collapsed on itself because of hundreds of years of constant warfare and irresponsible behavior of Roman emperors. And let's not forget the spiritual wickedness, sexual immorality, disparity between rich and poor, the ancient mystery religions, and Roman Catholicism merging itself together with the mystery religions. Roman Catholicism, with its doctrine of the Trinity, is pagan and bad all by itself. In fact, the ancient mystery religions and Greek philosophy, along with the lack of understanding of the dual nature of Christ, gave birth to Catholicism. But after Emperor and Pope Constantine I married the Catholic Church to the Roman Empire, Roman Catholicism absorbed more mystery religions and descended into outer darkness. All of these things caused the Roman Empire to fall. And the greatest sin of the empire was pride.

The state of Rome was gone, but the Roman Catholic Church remained. This is the beginning of the Dark Ages (AD 476–1000), especially in Western Europe. The east had its emperor, but Western Europe had the Catholic Church and a bunch of barbarian kings. Without the state of Rome to back them up, the Catholic Church was vulnerable. In fact, the Catholics were surrounded by Burgundians, Franks, Vandals, Visigoths, and other barbarian tribes. And these various tribes were mostly Arians.

The Catholic Church needed to convert the barbarians in order to maintain their power. So after a chain of events, the Catholics won over the Frankish King Clovis I (AD 481–511) in AD 496. He is one of the main ancestors of the Merovingian dynasty, which is one of the wealthiest and most powerful dynasties in today's world. Clovis I converted to Catholicism under the influence of his Catholic wife, Clotilda. This event brought the whole nation of Franks into the Catholic Church and eventually checked the spread of Arianism by the Ostrogoths. And throughout the Dark Ages, the Catholic Church would convert more prominent people and become more powerful. The Roman Catholic Church will become the government and rule the western world.

Prior to and after the fall of the Roman Empire, God's apostolic ekklesia waxed strong despite all the circumstances. For example, Pope Leo I martyred many of God's anointed tongue-talkers in AD 453. Once again, the Roman Catholics thought they were the true ekklesia of God. But if they were unable to convert someone, especially if that person was truly saved, then the Catholics would persecute or at worst kill the individual. Yeshua said that you will know them by their fruit. Despite much persecution coming their way, the saints continued to baptize sinners in the name of the Lord Jesus Christ. Scholar T. M. Lindsay wrote the following:

> The historian Socrates informs us that some of the more extreme Arians 'corrupted' baptism by using only the name of Christ in the formula; while injunctions to use the longer formula and punishments, including deposition, threatened to those who presumed to employ the shorter, which meet us in collections of ecclesiastical canons (*Apostolic Canons* 43, 50), prove that the practice of using the shorter formula existed in the 5th and 6th cents., at all events in the East.

Mr. Lindsay is saying that the saints were ordered by the Catholic Church to use the Catholic formula of baptism. The Catholics also threatened to punish the ekklesia for baptizing in the name of Jesus. But the saints of God throughout Europe chose to obey the Lord Jesus rather than men. As a result, God filled many sinners with the Holy Ghost, and they spoke in unknown tongues as the Spirit of Jesus gave utterance. Glory to Jesus in the highest!

The messianic community was still in the known world outside of Europe. For instance, the saints were in Africa during the kingdoms of Aksum (AD 100–940), Makuria (AD 340–1276), and Nobatia (AD 350–650) . Also, the saints continued to teach the apostle's doctrine in parts of Africa that were west and south of these kingdoms. In addition, the churches of Yeshua were still in ancient Arabia and Asia Minor. With the help of the Most High, the saints were still preaching the gospel of Jesus the Messiah in China before and after this nation established Buddhism as its state religion in AD 477. The churches were also flourishing in parts of ancient Russia. And the ekklesia was still winning souls for Christ in ancient Persia; souls were being saved while the Armenians were revolting against Persian rule from AD 481–484. The saints were triumphant on all three continents of the known world. So with their hearts and minds fixed on the coming of the Lord, God's original and primitive ekklesia marched triumphantly into the sixth century.

To be continued.

APPENDIX: TIMELINE

FIRST CENTURY
- AD 14—Emperor Gaius Julius Caesar Augustus, the first Roman emperor, died at the age of seventy-six. Tiberius became his successor.
- AD 30—Jesus Christ, our God made known in the flesh, died on the cross for the sins of the whole world. Then three days later, He got up from the grave. Fifty days later, the Day of Pentecost occurred. The Holy Ghost came upon Mary, the apostles, and about 120 disciples. The church age officially began.
- AD 34—Stephen, the first saint to be martyred, was stoned to death. Also, the Samaritans were converted to Christianity, and Deacon Philip converted the Ethiopian eunuch.
- AD 35—Saul of Tarsus, a.k.a. Paul, was converted to Christianity.
- AD 37–42—A saint of God took the apostle's doctrine to ancient Glastonbury, England.
- AD 39—Apostle Peter converts Cornelius and his household to the faith.
- AD 41—Emperor Caligula (AD 37–41) was assassinated; Claudius (AD 41–54) was made emperor of Rome.
- AD 44—The apostle James, John's brother, was martyred by Herod Agrippa I. Also, Herod Agrippa I died the same year.
- AD 45–50—James, the Lord's younger brother according to the flesh, wrote his epistle to the church.

- AD 47—Paul began his first missionary journey throughout the Roman Empire.
- AD 48–56—Paul wrote his letter to the churches in Galatia.
- AD 49—The ekklesia called its first church council in Jerusalem. Afterward, Paul began his second missionary journey throughout the Roman Empire.
- AD 50s—The apostle Thaddaeus (a.k.a. Judas) traveled to ancient Armenia and established the church in that area. Also, the apostle Thomas traveled to Malabar, India and established the ekklesia there.
- AD 51–52—Paul wrote his first and second epistles to the Thessalonians.
- AD 53—Paul began his third missionary journey throughout the Roman Empire.
- AD 54—Emperor Nero ascended to the throne. He was the first emperor to initiate a major persecution against God's church. Also, the apostle Philip was scourged and afterward crucified at Hierapolis.
- AD 55—Paul wrote his first letter to the Corinthian church.
- AD 55–59—The apostle Matthew wrote his gospel of Jesus Christ.
- AD 56—Paul finished his third missionary journey and wrote his second epistle to the Corinthians. Then, he wrote his letter to the Romans.
- AD 60—Luke wrote his version of the gospel of Jesus Christ.
- AD 60–62—Paul was imprisoned in Rome. During this period, Paul wrote his epistles to Philemon, the Colossians, Ephesians, and Philippians.
- AD 61—Luke wrote The Acts of the Holy Ghost, the original title of the Book of Acts, or Acts of the Apostles.
- AD 62—Paul wrote his first epistle to Timothy.
- AD 63—Paul wrote his pastoral epistle to Titus.

- AD 63–67—Someone, probably the apostle Paul, wrote the Epistle to the Hebrews.
- AD 64–67—The apostle Peter wrote his first epistle.
- AD 64–68—The disciple Mark wrote his version of the good news of Jesus the Messiah.
- AD 66–70—The Jewish Zealots led the Great Revolt against the Roman Empire.
- AD 67—Peter wrote his second epistle, and Paul wrote his second letter to Timothy. Also, both apostles were martyred (killed for their faith).
- AD 67–68—Jude, the Lord's younger brother according to the flesh, wrote his epistle to the saints of God.
- AD 68—Emperor Nero committed suicide.
- AD 69—Titus Flavius Vespasianus became the emperor of the Roman Empire.
- AD 70—The temple in Jerusalem was destroyed by the Romans.
- AD 74—The apostle Simon the Zealot was crucified.
- AD 80—During the reign of Emperor Titus, the Flavian Amphitheater, a.k.a. Colosseum, in Rome was completed.
- AD 81—Emperor Domitian ascended to the throne. He brought about the second major persecution against the saints in the Roman Empire.
- AD 85—The apostle John wrote his version of the gospel of Jesus Christ.
- AD 85–90—The apostle John wrote his three epistles to the saints of God. Also, the Old Testament was officially canonized by the Jews at Jamnia.
- AD 90–140—The post-apostolic age had begun, even though John was still alive. The most prominent leaders of the church were John, Clement of Rome, Hermas, Polycarp of Smyrna, and Ignatius of Antioch.

- AD 96–97—The apostle John was banished to the isle of Patmos. Also, John wrote the book of Revelations.
- AD 98—John was released from Patmos and returned to Ephesus. Also, Trajan became the emperor of the Roman Empire.
- AD 99–100—John fell asleep in Christ Jesus.

SECOND CENTURY

- AD 100—Clement of Rome suffered martyrdom. Also, the African Kingdom of Aksum had begun.
- AD 107—St. Ignatius of Antioch suffered martyrdom. (It is possible that he was martyred at a later date.) He was one of the many saints who died during Emperor Trajan's persecution.
- AD 117—Hadrian became the emperor of Rome after Trajan's death.
- AD 118—Emperor Hadrian allowed the Israelites to return to Jerusalem to rebuild the holy temple for the third time. But after he did this, Hadrian decided to change his mind. His action enraged the Jews. Another Jewish revolt against the Roman Empire was coming.
- AD 120—*The Shepherd of Hermas* was written.
- AD 123—The Jews organized guerilla forces and began launching surprise attacks against the Romans. This made life worse for all Jews in the empire.
- AD 125—Pseudo-Christian Gnosticism came on the scene. Gnostics mixed some fundamental Christian ideas and traditions with their basically non-Christian, pagan speculations and theories. In doing so, they denied Jesus's humanity and taught that all matter (including humanity) was evil. Famous Gnostics of the second century were Basilides, Carpocrates, Valentinus, Marcion, and Bardesanes.

- AD 130—A saint of old age witnessed to Justin Martyr in Ephesus. Justin refused his testimony. But he took the saint's advice and decided to search the Holy Scriptures on his own. This led to his false conversion to primitive Christianity.
- AD 130s—Justin searched the Scriptures, but he remained a Greek philosopher. He, and others like him, brought the earliest form of Catholicism into the ancient world.
- AD 130–180—During this period, the Greek apologists (Justin, Aristides, Athenagoras, Tatian, and Theophilus) came on the scene. Because of these men, defenses of the Catholic faith were developed. These included an authoritative leadership, a formal canon of scripture, and a systematic theology. The result was the institution of the ancient Catholic Church.
- AD 132–135—Shimon Bar-Kokhba led the Bar-Kokhba Revolt against the Roman Empire. Despite their efforts, the Jews suffered another crushing defeat by the Romans.
- AD 138—Antoninus Pius became the emperor of Rome.
- AD 140—Roman bishop Pius I was in Rome, Italy.
- AD 140s—Early in this decade, Justin went to Rome and started his own school of theology.
- AD 150—Justin Martyr wrote his first apology. It describes the ancient Catholic formula of baptism for the first time. Also, Tertullian was born.
- AD 154—Anicetus became the Catholic bishop of Rome.
- AD 156—Montanists claimed new revelation from God in addition to the revelations taught by Jews and Christians.
- AD 161—Marcus Aurelius became the emperor of Rome. He initiated another major persecution against all Christians in the Roman Empire. It's very probable that Polycarp of Smyrna was martyred during his reign.
- AD 165—Justin was martyred as a Catholic.

- AD 174—The Roman legions of Marcus Aurelius defeated the Quadi, a Germanic tribe.
- AD 175—Early ideas about purgatory, catechism, and confirmation seeped into Catholicism, which are adopted from the Orphic cult.
- AD 180—Irenaeus wrote *Adversus Haereses*, which is a five-volume series of books.
- AD 180–190—During this period, the Catechetical School of Alexandria was started. Pantaenus was the first head of this Catholic school in Egypt.
- AD 183—Roman Emperor Commodus escaped death at the hands of assassins who have attacked him at the instigation of his sister Lucilia and a large group of senators. He put many distinguished Romans to death on charges of being implicated in the conspiracy and puts others to death for no reason at all.
- AD 189—Plague (possibly smallpox) killed as many as two thousand people per day in Rome. Dying farmers were unable to harvest their crops, dying carters were not able to deliver what grain there was, and food shortages brought riots in the city. Also, Victor I became the Catholic bishop of Rome.
- AD 190—Praxeas traveled to Rome and established his own church there. We know for sure that he was preaching the gospel and teaching the apostle's doctrine in Rome. Also, Tertullian converted to Catholicism while he was in Rome.
- AD 193—Septimius Severus became the emperor of Rome.
- AD 199—Zephyrinus, a member of God's ekklesia, became the bishop of the Roman Catholic Church. The Catholics did not like him as their bishop. Also, Rome's war with Parthia ends following a second unsuccessful effort by Emperor Septimius Severus to capture the pro-Parthian city-state of Hatra in central Mesopotamia.

THIRD CENTURY

- AD 200—Clement of Alexandria became the head of the Catechetical School of Alexandria after Pantaenus's death. Also, the Jewish Talmudic law had its beginnings in the thirty-nine tractates of the Mishnah compiled by Palestinian scholar-patriarch Judah ha-Kadosh of Sepphoria. (Note: Catholicism would gain a wide following in this century, although many practicing Catholics would continue to worship the old Roman gods.)
- AD 202—Emperor Septimius Severus enacted a rigid law that forbade all Roman citizens to join Christianity and Judaism. Many saints and Catholics died during Severus's persecution.
- AD 207—Tertullian left the Catholic Church, joined the Montanists, and became the head of a small Montanist community in Carthage.
- AD 211—Emperor Severus died. Caracalla succeeded him as emperor.
- AD 215—Clement of Alexandria died. Origen succeeded him as the new head of the Catechetical School of Alexandria. Also, Sabellius of Libya came on the scene in Rome, Italy.
- AD 217—Zephyrinus died. Another saint of God named Callistus I succeeded him as bishop of Rome.
- AD 217–220—Hippolytus of Rome and his followers withdrew from the Catholic Church, caused the first schism in the Catholic Church's history, and made himself a rival bishop.
- AD 220—China's Wei dynasty would give official recognition to Daoism (Taoism) as its religious sect.
- AD 222—Callistus I was martyred. Urban I became the Roman bishop.
- AD 230—Urban I died. And then Pontian was elected bishop of the Catholic Church. After this happened, Hippolytus and

his followers ended their schism and rejoined the Catholic Church in Rome.
- AD 235–285—The Crisis of the Third Century occurred. During this period, the Roman Empire almost collapsed on itself. In fact, thirty emperors reigned during this fifty-year period. But of that number, only two died in their own bed. The rest were assassinated while Emperor Gordian I committed suicide.
- AD 249—Trajan Decius became the emperor of Rome.
- AD 250—Emperor Decius instituted the first wholesale persecution of Christians in an attempt to restore the religion and institutions of ancient Rome. Also, Commodian, a saint of God, became the bishop of his own church somewhere in North Africa.
- AD 251—Novatian, failing to be elected bishop of Rome, had himself consecrated bishop. He taught the heresy that sins committed after baptism cannot be forgiven, idolatry can never be pardoned, and baptism by aspersion (sprinkling) only. Novatian and his followers were excommunicated by a synod of bishops in Rome in 261.
- AD 252—The Council of Carthage decided that all newborn infants must be baptized within eight days.
- AD 253–260—Emperor Valerian persecuted the saints and Catholics during his reign.
- AD 254–257—Roman Catholic Bishop Stephen I declared baptism in the name of Jesus Christ to be valid. Cyprian of Carthage was not pleased.
- AD 255—Cyprian called a Council at Carthage in which thirty-one bishops denounced baptism in the name of Jesus. This is the first council in history where baptism in the name of Jesus was formally denounced.

- AD 258—Novatian died, but his schismatic church continued to thrive.
- AD 260—Roman Bishop Dionysius convened a synod at Rome to demand an explanation from Bishop Dionysius of Alexandria, who was charged with separating the members of the Trinity as three distinct deities (tritheism). Discussions at the synod about differing Greek and Roman interpretations of the same terms resolve the "affair of the two Dionysii."
- AD 267—Palmyra's Prince Odenaethus was assassinated along with his eldest son, evidently on orders from the Roman emperor Gallienus.
- AD 268—Roman Emperor Gallienus was killed by his own senior officers at Mediolanum (Milan) while besieging the pretender Aureolus, who surrendered in late summer or early fall and was slain in turn by the imperial guard. The Illyricum-born pretender, Marcus Aurelius Claudius, was charged with having murdered Gallienus (it will never be proven) and would reign until 270 as Claudius II.
- AD 270–275—Emperor Aurelian persecuted all Christians during his reign. When persecution under Aurelian ended, all Roman citizens still had to endure what was going on in the empire during the crisis.
- AD 277—Roman Emperor Probus liberated Gaul from the Franks and Alamanni, having traveled west across the Propontis and through the provinces of Thrace, Moesia, and Pannonia. He visited Rome to have his powers ratified by the Senate.
- AD 280—Forces of China's western Jin (Chin) dynasty Emperor Wudi wiped out survivors of the Three Kingdoms Period that ruled from 221 to 265 and reunified the north and south.
- AD 284—Diocletian ascended to the throne and reigned as emperor.

- AD 286–293—Emperor Diocletian established the Tetrarchy, which divided the empire into four regions to be ruled by a co-emperor. This Tetrarchy split the Roman Empire into two parts: east and west. Diocletian and Galerius ruled in the east while Constantius Chlorus and Maximian ruled in the west.
- AD 292—The Egyptians revolted against the rule of Rome, but Emperor Diocletian suppressed the uprising.
- AD 297—Persia's king Narses ousted Armenia's king Tiradates. When Emperor Diocletian sent his Thracian co-emperor Galerius Valerius Maximanus to confront Narses near Carrhae, the Roman forces were beaten back.
- AD 298—Roman co-emperor Galerius Valerius Maximanus obtained reinforcements, routed the Persian army, and forced Persia's king Narses to sign the Treaty of Nisibis, ceding some lands beyond the Tigris and affirming Roman supremacy over Armenia.

FOURTH CENTURY

- AD 301—Gregory the Illuminator (AD 257–331) baptized Tiridates III along with members of the royal court and upper class as Catholics. The same year Armenia became the first country to adopt Catholicism as its state religion. Due to Gregory's accomplishments, the saints of God reaped the whirlwind. Church buildings that belonged to God's messianic community were confiscated.
- AD 303—Emperor Diocletian initiated what is now called the Great Persecution against all who claimed to be followers of Christ.
- AD 305—Diocletian resigned as emperor due to illness and was succeeded by Galerius. After this happened, the Great Persecution against God's elect and the Catholics intensified, especially in the east.

- AD 306—Constantine I became the emperor of the west when his father Constantius died.
- AD 310—Arius, a priest in Alexandria, began teaching a Trinitarian heresy which was named after him, Arianism.
- AD 311—Emperor Galerius died in May after the despot Maxentius had driven him out of Italy. Emperor Constantine had plotted to kill his rivals and began a march on Rome. Also, the Great Persecution continued.
- AD 312—The Battle of Milvian Bridge (or *Saxa Rubra*), four miles north of Rome on October 28, gave Emperor Constantine a victory over the despot Maxentius. He crossed the Alps via Mont Cénis, the bridge collapsed, many men drowned, and Constantine killed Maxentius the next day, making himself absolute master of the Western Roman Empire.
- AD 313—Edict of Milan was issued by Constantine. As a result, Catholicism and Primitive Christianity were tolerated in the Roman Empire. The Great Persecution was finally over. Also, Constantine formed an alliance with eastern emperor Licinius I.
- AD 314—Constantine got involved in the dispute between the Catholics and Donatists by calling the Council of Arles because they were not getting anywhere close to resolving their issues.
- AD 317—Constantine sent troops to deal with the Donatists in Carthage. So the Catholics, who had come out of persecution, were now persecuting the Donatists. This decision by the emperor resulted in banishments but ultimately failed.
- AD 318—Arius caused the Arian controversy, which began because of a disagreement between him and his bishop, Alexander. Arianism was very troublesome to Roman Catholicism and at one point almost two-thirds of the bishops had embraced it.

- AD 320—The Gupta dynasty began to unify northern India after five centuries of division. Chandragupta, king of Magaha, founded the dynasty.
- AD 321—Emperor Constantine withdrew his troops and ended the persecutions against the Donatists. Also, Constantine issued a proclamation on July 3 making Sunday a day of rest throughout the Roman Empire. Jews continued to observe the Sabbath on Saturday, and Constantine himself continued to worship the ancient Roman sun god, Apollo, despite his acceptance of Catholicism.
- AD 324—Licinius was persecuting the ekklesia and Catholics in the east. As a result, Constantine and his army met Licinius and his army on the battlefield. From ancient Adrianople to Chrysopolis, Constantine pursued his rival. At Chrysopolis, Constantine and his army annihilated Licinius's army. Constantine won sole rulership of the Roman Empire.
- AD 325—Emperor Constantine called the Council of Nicaea. The Council condemned Arianism, set the date for Easter, and declared that God the Father and God the Son were of the same substance. Arius was exiled.
- AD 326—Constantine traveled to Rome to celebrate the twentieth anniversary of his accession. But while en route at Pola, he executes his older son, Crispus Caesar, on charges of trying to have sex with his stepmother. Constantine's second wife, Fausta, has borne him three younger sons; she has persuaded him to eliminate his son by his first wife, and Constantine has Fausta herself suffocated in her bath later in the year.
- AD 328—Alexandria's patriarch Bishop Alexander died and was succeeded by his deacon Athanasius, who will gain support from the Roman Bishops at Rome in his persecution of Arian "heretics."
- AD 330—Constantine built the original St. Peter's Basilica.

- AD 335—Arianism triumphed over Catholicism at the Council of Tyre.
- AD 336—Arius died.
- AD 337—Emperor Constantine submitted to Catholic baptism and died.
- AD 340—The African Kingdom of Makuria had begun.
- AD 341—Persecuted Catholics, and possibly the saints of God, in Mesopotamia died by the thousands as the co-emperor Constantius reversed the tolerant policies of his late father.
- AD 346—Roman co-emperor Constans used his influence to secure the return of the former Alexandrian patriarch Athanasius to Egypt, where the next ten years will be a period of peace and prosperity in which Athanasius will compile documents relating to his expulsion and return under the title *Apology against the Arians*.
- AD 350—Roman co-emperor Constans was murdered in Gaul; his military commander Magnentius engineered a coup d'état and usurped the western empire, and the death of Constans precipitated a period of civil war. Also, the African kingdom of Nobatia had begun.
- AD 352—By this date, Ash Wednesday, Lent, and Mass were in use in the Catholic Church. Also, chantings started.
- AD 353—The Roman legions of Constantius II defeated the usurper Magnentius, who commited suicide in Gaul on August 11 in order to avoid capture. Constantius II became sole emperor and will reign until his death in 361.
- AD 361—Catholics of Constantinople confiscated the Apostolic Pentecostal church buildings in Cappadocia.
- AD 369—The new Visigothic king Fritigern adopted Arianism, which was favored by Roman Emperor Valens that rejected the doctrine of the Trinity. His rival Athanaric would be the last

Gothic king to follow the traditional Germanic pagan religion of Asatru.
- AD 373—Athanasius died. Also, Buddhism came into Korea from China.
- AD 375—Roman Emperor Gratian declined to accept the title Pontifex Maximus, believing its pagan origins unsuited to a Catholic monarch. But the bishop of Rome, Damasus I, appropriated the title Pontifex Maximus to himself. Thus the religio-political title of the Caesars passed without objection to the papacy.
- AD 380—The text of 1 John 5:7 was expanded by the Catholics first in Spain first.
- AD 381—Emperor Theodosius I convened the Council of Constantinople. Also, Roman Catholicism was made the official religion of the Roman Empire.
- AD 382—Jerome, a Catholic father, began his work of making a better Latin version of the Old and New Testament. First, he translated the New Testament Scriptures into Latin by correcting the *Vetus Latina*.
- AD 387—Augustine converted to Catholicism.
- AD 390—Jerome began his work of translating the Hebrew Old Testament into Latin. Also, Emperor Theodosius killed seven thousand saints of God at Thessalonica.
- AD 393—The synods of Hippo accepted the Holy Bible as well as the books of the Apocrypha into their canon.
- AD 394—The Battle of Frigidus occurred. This battle was brutal, but Theodosius defeated Arbogast and his army. This victory made Theodosius the sole ruler of the Roman Empire. He is the last Roman emperor to be the sole ruler of the Roman Empire.

- AD 395—Theodosius I died. Afterward, the Roman Empire is permanently split into the eastern and western empire.
- AD 397—The synods of Carthage also accepted the Holy Bible as well as the books of the Apocrypha into the Catholic canon of the Bible.

FIFTH CENTURY

- AD 401—Visigoths penetrated the northern defenses of Italy and had begun to ravage the countryside.
- AD 402—There were only about sixty-four Catholic bishops in Africa and Asia Minor combined.
- AD 404—The Council of Carthage condemned Donatism. The Donatist controversies led to the clarification of a number of important questions for the Catholic Church—such as the efficacy of the sacraments *ex opere operato*; the nature of the Church, of schism, of heresy; and the relations between Church and State. Also, Augustine wrote against Donatism.
- AD 405—Jerome completed his Latin Vulgate. The Apocrypha (in the Latin language) was also included in Jerome's Latin version of the Bible.
- AD 408—Roman Emperor Honorius issued a decree against his barbarian General Stilicho. This led to Stilicho's death.
- AD 410—King Alaric I and his Visigoths sacked the great city of Rome. For the first time in eight hundred years, Rome itself was sacked by an enemy.
- AD 412—Visigoth forces moved from Italy into southern Gaul under the leadership of Atawulf (Ataulf), brother-in-law of the late Alaric.
- AD 415—Visigoths invaded the Iberian Peninsula early in the year and began to conquer territory taken previously by the Vandals; the Visigoths were driven out of Gaul, and their chieftain Atawulf (Ataulf) was assassinated at Barcelona.

- AD 418—The Catholic Church reasserted its teaching on infant baptism at the Council of Carthage. The council stated that infants must be baptized so that sin may be remitted.
- AD 419—Ancient Toulouse, France, was not only a Gothic state, it was protected as an apostolic pentecostal stronghold.
- AD 421—Eastern Roman emperor Theodosius II sent his army against Persia's new king Bahram V, who had been persecuting all who claim to worship Jesus Christ.
- AD 428—The patriarch of Constantinople Nestorius preached a new doctrine that will be called Nestorianism. It made a distinction between the divine and human natures of Jesus but came under immediate attack from Pope Celestine I and Cyril of Alexandria.
- AD 431—The Council of Ephesus occurred. Catholic bishops declared that Mary is the Mother of God.
- AD 443—The Huns, under the command of Attila, defeated Byzantine forces under the command of Flavius Ardaburius Aspar outside Constantinople.
- AD 444—A pestilence called the bubonic plague struck the British Isles and made the country vulnerable to conquest.
- AD 449—The Second Council of Ephesus in Asia Minor ended August 8 by backing the Monophysite patriarch of Alexandria, who taught the Eutychianist philosophy that the incarnate Christ is of a single, divine nature. The patriarch enjoyed the support of Egypt's monastic movement, but the council's decision was a rebuff to Pope Leo I.
- AD 451—The Ecumenical Council of Chalcedon condemned the heresy of Monophytism, which denied the humanity of Christ by holding that He had only one nature (the divine).
- AD 452—Attila the Hun invaded northern Italy in a renewed effort to obtain the hand of Honoria, sister of Emperor Valentinian III, who had been obliged by her brother to marry

the senator Flavius Bassus Herculanus and kept under close guard. Also, Attila sacked Padua, Verona, and other cities, killing their inhabitants or taking them into slavery.
- AD 453—Attila the Hun died on his wedding night. Also, Pope Leo I martyred many members of God's ekklesia.
- AD 455—The city of Rome was sacked again by Vandal barbarians from North Africa.
- AD 456—The Battle of Placentia in northern Italy ended in defeat for the Roman Emperor Avitus, who was forced to abdicate. His rebel general Ricimer, of the Suevian tribe, attempted to rule through a puppet Emperor, Majorian.
- AD 461—The puppet western emperor Majorian was deposed on August 2 after making a show of independence and was killed by the barbarian general Ricimer who installed him. Ricimer replaced him with Libius Severus, another puppet emperor.
- AD 465—Ricimer had his puppet Emperor Severus assassinated. After the emperor's death, Ricimer ruled the west for eighteen months.
- AD 467—Through Eastern Emperor Leo, Anthemius replaced Ricimer as the emperor of the west.
- AD 469—The Vatican made a pact with the Salian Frankish king Childeric I, agreeing to call him "the new Constantine" on condition that he accepted conversion to Catholicism.
- AD 472—The barbarian general Ricimer killed the Roman Emperor Anthemius and replaced him with Olybrius. Ricimer died August 19. The Burgundian general Gundobad assumed command of the western army. Olybrius died November 2, and the Western Roman Empire was without an emperor for several months.
- AD 473—The Burgundian general Gundobad nominated Glycerius as western Roman emperor.

- AD 474—Eastern Emperor Leo I died of dysentery at Constantinople January 18 at seventy-three. He was succeeded by Zeno. Also, Julius Nepos deposed Glycerius and became emperor of the west.
- AD 475—Orestes took control of the western empire's government at Ravenna and forced Emperor Nepos to flee by ship to Dalmatia. Afterward, Nepos spent the rest of his life in exile. Then Orestes elevated his son Romulus Augustus to the throne in Rome.
- AD 476—Odovacer went to Ravenna to confront western emperor Augustus. At the age of twelve, Romulus Augustus was deposed by Odovacer and exiled to Castellum Lucullanum in Campania. He was the last emperor of the west. So the Dark Ages began in Western Europe.
- AD 477—China established Buddhism as its state religion.
- AD 481—The Armenians began their revolt against Persian rule.
- AD 486—The Battle of Noviodnum (Soissons) ended in victory for the Frankish king Clovis I, now twenty-one, who crushed the kingdom of the Roman Syagorius in northern Gaul.
- AD 493—The Herulian leader Odovacar surrendered the city of Ravenna on March 3 after a three-year siege by Theodoric, who invited Odovacar to dinner and had him murdered.
- AD 496—King Clovis I converted to Roman Catholicism under the influence of his Catholic wife, Clotilda.

BIBLIOGRAPHY

Answers.com. "First Century." Retrieved May 24, 2012. http://www.answers.com/topic/first-century.

Answers.com. "Second Century." Retrieved May 24, 2012. http://www.answers.com/topic/2nd-century.

Answers.com. "Third Century." Retrieved May 24, 2012. http://www.answers.com/topic/3rd-century.

The Crisis of the Third Century. Retrieved June 18, 2011. http://isthmia.osu.edu/teg/50501/4.htm.

Answers.com. "Fourth Century." Retrieved May 24, 2012. http://www.answers.com/topic/4th-century.

Answers.com. "Fifth Century." Retrieved March 26, 2012. http://www.answers.com/topic/5th-century.

"Alaric I." *Wikipedia.* Retrieved January 2, 2012. http:// en.wikipedia.org/wiki/Alaric_I.

Arendzen, J. "Marcellus of Ancyra." *The Catholic Encyclopedia.* New York: Robert Appleton Company, 1910. Retrieved November 28, 2011. http://www.newadvent.org/cathen/ 09642a.htm.

"Arius." *Wikipedia.* Retrieved August 19, 2011. http:// en.wikipedia.org/wiki/Arius.

Arnold, M. M. *Apostolic History Outline.* Cincinnati: Bethesda Ministries, Inc., 2000.

"Athanasius of Alexandria." *Wikipedia.* Retrieved November 28, 2011. http://en.wikipedia.org/wiki/Athanasius_of_Alexandria.

"Athenagoras of Athens." *Wikipedia*. Retrieved September 13, 2010. http://en.wikipedia.org/wiki/Athenagoras_of_Athens.

B., J. C. "Marcellus of Ancyra." Retrieved September 20, 2011. http://www.fourthcentury.com/index.php/ marcellus-of-ancyra/.

Bacchus, F. J. Pantænus. *The Catholic Encyclopedia*. New York: Robert Appleton Company, 1911. Retrieved December 31, 2010. http://www.newadvent.org/cathen/11446b.htm.

Baird, W. "The Acts of the Apostles." *The Interpreter's One-Volume Commentary on the Bible*. Nashville: Abingdon, 1971.

Barry, W. "Arius." *The Catholic Encyclopedia*. New York: Robert Appleton Company, 1907. Retrieved November 12, 2011. http://www.newadvent.org/cathen/01718a.htm.

Benario, H. W. "Nero (54-68 AD) ." *An Online Encyclopedia of Roman Rulers*. November 10, 2006. Retrieved May 18, 2010. http://www.roman-emperors.org/nero.htm.

Bernard, D. K. *The Oneness of God: Series in Pentecostal Theology, Volume 1*. May 10, 2000. Retrieved April 22, 2011. http:// www.newlifeupc.org/wp-content/uploads/online-books/ oneness/One-Top.html.

Bernard, D. K. *The New Birth: Series in Pentecostal Theology, Volume 2*. Retrieved March 3, 2011. http://ourworld. compuserve.com/homepages/pentecostal/New-Top.htm.

Bonocore, M. *The Title Pontifex Maximus*. Retrieved September 20, 2011. http://www.philvaz.com/apologetics/a104.htm.

Bradshaw, R. *Irenaeus of Lyons (c. 155—c. 202)*. Retrieved September 14, 2010. http://www.earlychurch.org.uk/ irenaeus.php.

Bradshaw, R. *Justin Martyr (c.100—c.165)*. Retrieved August 22, 2010. http://www.earlychurch.org.uk/justin.php.

Bradshaw, R. *Theophilus of Antioch (Later second Century)*. Retrieved August 29, 2010. http://www.earlychurch.org. uk/theophilus.php.

Brom, R. H. Trinitarian Baptism. *Catholic Answers*. August 4, 2004. Retrieved November 5, 2010. http://www.catholic. com/tracts/trinitarian-baptism.

Bromiley, G. W. *The International Standard Bible Encyclopedia*. 1 vol. Grand Rapids: W.B. Eerdmans, 1979.

C., F. C. *Encyclopedia Britannica*. 11 ed. 3 vols. New York: Cambridge at the University Press, 1910.

Catechetical School of Alexandria. *Wikipedia*. Retrieved November 5, 2010. http://en.wikipedia.org/wiki/Catechetical_School_of_Alexandria.

CH101—The Fourth Century. *Early Church History— CH 101*. Retrieved August 11, 2011. http://www. churchhistory101.com/century4-p3.php.

Chapman, J. Pope Callistus I. *The Catholic Encyclopedia*. New York: Robert Appleton Company, 1908. Retrieved November 5, 2010. http://www.newadvent.org/ cathen/03183d.htm.

Chapman, J. St. Cyprian of Carthage. *The Catholic Encyclopedia*. New York: Robert Appleton Company, 1908. Retrieved July 16, 2011. http://www.newadvent. org/cathen/04583b.htm.

Chapman, J. Robber Council of Ephesus. *The Catholic Encyclopedia*. New York: Robert Appleton Company, 1909. Retrieved February 18, 2012. http://www. newadvent.org/cathen/05495a.htm.

Chapman, J. Paul of Samosata. *The Catholic Encyclopedia*. New York: Robert Appleton Company, 1911. Retrieved August 8, 2011. http://www.newadvent.org/cathen/11589a.htm.

Chapman, J. Catholic Encyclopedia (1913)/Praxeas. *Wikisource*. Retrieved May 14, 2011. http://en.wikisource. org/wiki/Catholic_Encyclopedia_%281913%29/Praxeas. *Christian Persecution*. Retrieved May 11, 2010. http://www.unrv.com/culture/christian-persecution.php.

Clement of Alexandria (c. 150–c. 211 AD). *ReligionFacts*. November 21, 2004. Retrieved November 10, 2010. http://www.religionfacts.com/christianity/people/ clement_alexandria.htm.

Clement of Alexandria. *Wikipedia*. Retrieved January 14, 2011. http://en.wikipedia.org/wiki/Clement_of_Alexandria.

Closson, D. The Council of Nicea. *Probe Ministries*, 2003. Retrieved August 19, 2011. http://www.probe.org/site/c.fdKEIMNsEoG/b.4225757/k.575C/The_Council_of_ Nicea.htm.

Constantine the Great. *Wikipedia*. Retrieved August 16, 2011. http://en.wikipedia.org/wiki/Constantine_I.

Copes, W. *Historical Development of the Trinitarian Mode of Baptism*. Retrieved July 30, 2011. http://www. pentecostalsonline.org/one.html.

Council of Chalcedon. *Wikipedia*. Retrieved March 15, 2012. http://en.wikipedia.org/wiki/Council_of_Chalcedon.

Craft, D. *The Apostle John During and After Christ's Passion*. Retrieved May 6, 2010. http://www.therowaninitiative. org/?the_apostle_john_during.

Cyprian. *Wikipedia*. Retrieved July 5, 2011. http:// en.wikipedia.org/wiki/Cyprian.

Dau, W. H. T. *The International Standard Bible Encyclopedia*. 1 vol. Grand Rapids: W.B. Eerdmans, 1979.

Diocletian and the Great Persecution. *AncientWorlds*. April 28, 2005. Retrieved August 15, 2011. http://www. ancientsites.com/aw/Article/553109.

Donahue, J. Titus Flavius Vespasianus (AD 69–79). *An Online Encyclopedia of Roman Rulers*. September 23, 2004. Retrieved May 10, 2010. http://www.roman-emperors. org/vespasia.htm.

Donatism. Retrieved August 18, 2011. http://www.philtar. ac.uk/encyclopedia/christ/early/donat.html.

Donatism. *Wikipedia*. Retrieved August 18, 2011. http:// en.wikipedia.org/wiki/Donatism.

Emperors and the Colosseum. 2008. Retrieved June 15, 2011. http://www.roman-colosseum.info/colosseum/emperors -and-the-colosseum.htm.

Firmilian. *Wikipedia*. Retrieved July 23, 2011. http:// en.wikipedia.org/ wiki/Firmilian.

First Council of Ephesus. *Wikipedia*. Retrieved March 23, 2012. http:// en.wikipedia.org/wiki/First_Council_of_ Ephesus.

First Council of Nicaea. *Wikipedia*. Retrieved October 8, 2011. http:// en.wikipedia.org/wiki/First_Council_of_Nicaea.

Fox's Book of Martyrs Chapter II. Retrieved May 13, 2010. http://www.ccel.org/f/foxe/martyrs/fox102.htm.

Fox's Book of Martyrs. Retrieved May 16, 2010. http://www. ccel.org/f/foxe/martyrs/fox101.htm.

Furnish, V. P. "Paul to the Galatians." *The Interpreter's One-Volume Commentary on the Bible*. The Letter of Nashville: Abingdon, 1971.

Gill, N. S. Tetrarchy. *Ancient / Classical History*. Retrieved July 3, 2011. http://ancienthistory.about.com/od/rome empire/g/tetrarchy.htm.

Glycerius. *Wikipedia*. Retrieved March 25, 2012. http:// en.wikipedia.org/wiki/Glycerius.

Gregory the Illuminator. *Wikipedia*. Retrieved May 28, 2012. http:// en.wikipedia.org/wiki/Gregory_the_Illuminator.

Gundobad. *Wikipedia*. Retrieved March 25, 2012. http:// en.wikipedia.org/wiki/Gundobad.

HA., A. X. *Encyclopedia Britannica*. 11 ed. 26 vols. New York: Cambridge at the University Press, 1910.

Havey, F. Clement of Alexandria. *The Catholic Encyclopedia*. New York: Robert Appleton Company, 1908. Retrieved April 28, 2011. http://www.newadvent.org/ cathen/04045a.htm.

Healy, P. Tatian. *The Catholic Encyclopedia* . New York: Robert Appleton Company, 1912. Retrieved September 3, 2010. http://www.newadvent.org/cathen/14464b.htm.

Hill, P. J. *New Catholic Encyclopedia*. 2 vols. New York: McGraw-Hill, 1967.

Hippolytus of Rome. *Wikipedia*. Retrieved November 4, 2010. http:// en.wikipedia.org/wiki/Hippolytus_of_Rome.

His Conversion. *Chapter 2, Justin Martyr: Convert from Heathendom.* Retrieved August 2, 2010. http://www.prca. org/books/portraits/martyr.htm.

Huston, D. A. *Oneness of God.* Retrieved January 21, 2012. http://the1favorites.tripod.com/id30.html.

Hutagalung, S. Christian Martyrs: Ten Persecutions Under Ten Roman Emperors. *My Study Light,* 2008. Retrieved August 8, 2010. http://www.mystudylight.com/miscella neous/miscellaneous.htm.

Hutagalung, S. Christian Martyrs: Ten Persecutions Under Ten Roman Emperors. *My Study Light,* 2008. Retrieved June 8, 2010. http://www.mystudylight.com/ miscellaneous/christian_martyrs_part_2.htm.

Ignatius of Antioch. Retrieved March 3, 2012. http://www. nndb.com/people/718/000094436/.

Ignatius of Antioch. *Wikipedia.* Retrieved August 26, 2010. http://en.wikipedia.org/wiki/Ignatius_of_Antioch.

Age of Antiquiry. "Rome: The Rise and Fall of an Empire–Episode 10: Constantine the Great (Documentary)". Filmed [February 2014]. YouTube video, 43:41. Posted [February 2014]. https://www.youtube.com/ watch?v=qcrYkk6Zd8I.

Age Of Antiquity. "Rome: The Rise and Fall of an Empire— Episode 11: The Barbarian General (Documentary)". Filmed [February 2014]. YouTube video, 43:32. Posted [February 2014]. https://www.youtube.com/ watch?v=A6Lhkm__pVU.

Age of Antiquity. "Rome: The Rise and Fall of an Empire— Episode 12: The Puppet Master (Documentary)". Filmed [February 2014]. YouTube video, 43:30. Posted [February 2014]. https://www.youtube.com/ watch?v=oPsXZGyqJ5o.

Age Of Antiquity. "Rome: The Rise and Fall of an Empire— Episode 13: The Last Emperor (Documentary)". Filmed [February 2014]. YouTube video, 43:29. Posted [February 2014]. https://www.youtube.com/ watch?v=uVP6wiwwnO4.

Introduction—Book of Revelation. Retrieved May 11, 2010. http://bibleprobe.com/revelation.htm.

Irenaeus. *Wikipedia.* Retrieved September 15, 2010. http://en.wikipedia.org/wiki/Irenaeus.

Jeffrey, G. R. The Martyrdom of the Apostles. *The Signature of God.* Retrieved May 16, 2010. http://www.bibleprobe.com/apostles.htm.

Jensen, I. L. *Jensen's Survey of the New Testament.* Chicago: Moody Publishers, 1981.

Jerome. *Wikipedia.* Retrieved January 26, 2012. http://en.wikipedia.org/wiki/Jerome.

Johnson, B. W. Chronology of Acts and the Epistles, The People's New Testament. *Blue Bible Letter.* April 1, 2002. Retrieved May 25, 2012. http://www.blueletterbible.org/ study/pnt/pnt02.cfm.

Julius Nepos. *Wikipedia.* Retrieved March 25, 2012. http://en.wikipedia.org/wiki/Julius_Nepos.

Jungmann, J. A. *New Catholic Encyclopedia.* 2 vols. New York: McGraw-Hill, 1967.

K., G. *Encyclopedia Britannica.* 11 ed. 15 vols. 15 New York: Cambridge at the University Press, 1910.

Kilkenny, N. Caesar is Pope!! *Emperor Constantine Was the First Pope!!* 2008. Retrieved August 13, 2011. http://www.reformation.org/pope-constantine.html.

Kingdom of Makuria. *Wikipedia.* Retrieved March 25, 2012. http://en.wikipedia.org/wiki/Makurian_kingdom.

Kirby, P. Tertullian. *Early Christian Writings.* 1996. Retrieved November 5, 2010. http://www.earlychristianwritings.com/text/tertullian17.html.

Kirby, P. Diatessaron. *Early Christian Writings.* 2006. Retrieved September 3, 2010. http://www.earlychristianwritings.com/text/diatessaron.html.

Kirby, P. Historical Jesus Theories. *Early Christian Writings*. Retrieved July 9, 2010. http://www.earlychristianwritings. com/text/1clement-hoole.html.

Kirby, P. Justin Martyr. *Early Christian Writings*. Retrieved August 24, 2010. http://www.earlychristianwritings.com/text/justinmartyr-firstapology.html.

Kirby, P. Justin Martyr. *Early Christian Writings*. Retrieved August 27, 2010. http://www.earlychristianwritings. com/text/justinmartyr-dialoguetrypho.html.

Kirby, P. The Apology of Aristides the Philosopher. *Early Christian Writings*. Retrieved August 29, 2010. http:// www.earlychristianwritings.com/text/aristides-kay.html.

Kirby, P. The Shepherd of Hermas. *Early Christian Writings*. Retrieved July 25, 2010. http://www.earlychristian writings.com/text/shepherd.html.

Kirsch, J.P. Pope St. Pontian. *The Catholic Encyclopedia*. New York: Robert Appleton Company, 1911. Retrieved November 5, 2010. http://www.newadvent.org/cathen/ 12229b.htm.

Kirsch, J.P. Pope St. Zephyrinus. *The Catholic Encyclopedia*. New York: Robert Appleton Company, 1912. Retrieved October 22, 2010. http://www.newadvent.org/cathen/ 15756c.htm.

Knott, R. *Apostolic Church History*. Retrieved November 18, 2010. www.godsguarantees.com/church_history.pdf.

Kramer, H. Crisis of the Third Century. *ACTA ACCLA*. December, 2004. Retrieved May 20, 2011. http://www. accla.org/actaaccla/kramer.html.

Lebreton, J. St. Justin Martyr. *The Catholic Encyclopedia*. New York: Robert Appleton Company, 1910. Retrieved August 20, 2010. http://www.newadvent.org/cathen/08580c. htm.

Leclercq, H. The First Council of Nicaea. *The Catholic Encyclopedia*. New York: Robert Appleton Company, 1911. Retrieved November 1, 2011. http://www. newadvent.org/cathen/11044a.htm.

Lindsay, T. M. *The International Standard Bible Encyclopedia*. 1 vol. Grand Rapids: W.B. Eerdmans, 1979.

List of Roman Emperors. *Wikipedia*. Retrieved July 28, 2010. http://en.wikipedia.org/wiki/List_of_Roman_Emperors.

Majorian. *Wikipedia*. Retrieved March 25, 2012. http://en.wikipedia.org/wiki/Majorian.

Mueller, H. *New Catholic Encyclopedia*. 2 vols. New York: McGraw-Hill, 1967.

Murphy, F. X. *New Catholic Encyclopedia*. 3 vols. New York: McGraw-Hill, 1967.

Norwood, F. A. "The Early History of the Church." *The Interpreter's One-Volume Commentary on the Bible*. Nashville: Abingdon, 1971.

Novatian. *Wikipedia*. Retrieved July 7, 2011. http://en.wikipedia.org/wiki/Novatian.

Pagan Sun Worship and Catholicism Celebrating the Risen Sun. *Bible Light*. Retrieved September 18, 2010. http://biblelight.net/easter.htm.

Pantaenus. *Wikipedia*. Retrieved November 15, 2010, from http://en.wikipedia.org/wiki/Pantaenus.

Parthian Religion. Retrieved September 28, 2010. http://persianempire.info/ParthianReligion.htm.

Paul of Samosata. *Wikipedia*. Retrieved August 10, 2011. http://en.wikipedia.org/wiki/Paul_of_Samosata.

Persecution of Christians in the Roman Empire. *Wikipedia*. Retrieved May 25, 2011. http://en.wikipedia.org/wiki/Persecution_of_Christians_in_the_Roman_Empire.

Peterson, J.B. Athenagoras. *The Catholic Encyclopedia*. New York: Robert Appleton Company, 1907. Retrieved September 4, 2010. http://www.newadvent.org/cathen/02042b.htm.

Peyton, H. A. *A History of Oneness Throughout the Centuries (Baptism in Jesus Name, the Godhead in Christ)*. Retrieved August 2,

2010. http://doctrinesofchrist.com/A%20 History%20of%20 Oneness%20throughout%20the%20 Centuries.pdf.

Pope Anicetus. *Wikipedia*. Retrieved August 30, 2010. http:// en.wikipedia.org/wiki/Pope_Anicetus.

Pope Callixtus I. *Wikipedia*. Retrieved November 5, 2010. http:// en.wikipedia.org/wiki/Pope_Callixtus_I.

Pope Cornelius. *Wikipedia*. Retrieved July 5, 2011. http:// en.wikipedia.org/wiki/Pope_Cornelius.

Pope Telesphorus. *Wikipedia*. Retrieved August 25, 2010. http:// en.wikipedia.org/wiki/Pope_Telesphorus.

Portalié, E. Life of St. Augustine of Hippo. *The Catholic Encyclopedia*. New York: Robert Appleton Company, 1907. Retrieved January 31, 2012. http://www.newadvent. org/cathen/02084a.htm.

Reign of Terror. Retrieved May 11, 2010. http://www.unrv. com/early-empire/reign-of-terror.php.

Reumann, J. "The Transmission of the Biblical Text." *The Interpreter's One-Volume Commentary on the Bible*. Nashville: Abingdon, 1971.

Richard, R. L. *New Catholic Encyclopedia*. 14 vols. New York: McGraw-Hill, 1967.

Ricimer. *Wikipedia*. Retrieved March 25, 2012. http:// en.wikipedia.org/wiki/Ricimer.

Ritchie, S. Trinitarian Contradictions and Oneness Theology in Early Church History. *The Essentiality of Oneness Theology. Does It Matter How You Were Baptized?* Retrieved July 11, 2010. http:// www.apostolic.edu/apostolicpillar/ articles/baptism.html.

Romulus Augustus. *Wikipedia*. Retrieved March 25, 2012. http:// en.wikipedia.org/wiki/Romulus_Augustus.

Sabellius. *Wikipedia*. Retrieved November 5, 2010. http:// en.wikipedia.org/wiki/Sabellius.

Sack of Rome (455). *Wikipedia*. Retrieved March 25, 2012. http:// en.wikipedia.org/wiki/Sack_of_Rome_%28455%29. Schaefer, F. Council of Chalcedon. *The Catholic Encyclopedia*. New York: Robert

Appleton Company, 1908. Retrieved February 20, 2012. http://www.newadvent.org/cathen/ 03555a.htm.

Schoenberg, S. The Bar-Kokhba Revolt (132–135 Ce). *Jewish Virtual Library*. Retrieved July 25, 2010. http://www. jewishvirtuallibrary.org/jsource/Judaism/revolt1.html.

Scrum, D. S. ARIUS (b. ca. 250 AD–d. 336 A.D.). *The New Schaff-Herzog Encyclopedia of Religious Knowledge, Philip Schaff Vol. I*. Retrieved September 20, 2011. http://www. tlogical.net/bioarius.htm.

Second Council of Ephesus. *New World Encyclopedia*, February 21, 2009. Retrieved March 24, 2012. http://www. newworldencyclopedia.org/entry/Second_Council_of_Ephesus.

Shepherd, M. H., Jr. "The First Letter of John." *The Interpreter's One-Volume Commentary on the Bible*. Nashville: Abingdon, 1971.

Silberman, L. H. "The Making of the Old Testament Canon." *The Interpreter's One-Volume Commentary on the Bible*. Nashville: Abingdon, 1971.

Slick, M. Donatism. *Christian Apologetics & Research Ministry*. Retrieved August 16, 2011. http://carm.org/donatism.

St. Irenaeus of Lyons (d. 202 A.D.). *ReligionFacts*. December 17, 2004. Retrieved September 15, 2010. http://www. religionfacts.com/christianity/people/irenaeus.htm.

St. Zephyrinus. *Defending the Faith*. Retrieved November 4, 2010. http://www.cfpeople.org/Books/Pope/popep15.htm.

Standish, C., & Standish, R. The Crown of the Caesars Passes to the Papacy. *Two Beasts, Three Deadly Wounds, and Fourteen Popes*. 2001. Retrieved May 28, 2012. http:// www.sundaylaw.net/books/other/standish/twobeasts/ tb02.htm.

Stern, D. H. *Complete Jewish Bible*. Clarksville: Jewish New Testament Publications, 1998.

Sullivan, J. The Athanasian Creed. *The Catholic Encyclopedia*. New York: Robert Appleton Company, 1907. Retrieved March 20, 2012. http://www.newadvent.org/ cathen/02033b.htm.

Sundberg, A. C., Jr. "The Making of the New Testament Canon." *The Interpreter's One-Volume Commentary on the Bible*. Nashville: Abingdon, 1971.

Synod of Arles. *Wikipedia*. Retrieved August 18, 2011. http://en.wikipedia.org/wiki/Council_of_Arles.

The Church: Its Beginning, Success, Failures. *To Tell You The Whole Truth about the Church and the Holy Bible*. 1996. Retrieved May 20, 2012. http://www.scborromeo.org/ truth/truth.pdf.

The Meaning of Numbers: The Number 50. Retrieved September 18, 2009. http://www.biblestudy.org/bibleref/meaning-of-numbers-in-bible/50.html.

The Third Ecumenical Council. *The Ecumenical Councils*. Retrieved March 23, 2012. http://www.fromdeathtolife.org/chistory/councils.html#ec3.

The World Book Dictionary. 1 vol. Chicago, IL: World Book, Inc., 1992.

The World Book Dictionary. 2 vols. Chicago, IL: World Book, Inc., 1992.

Theodosius I. *Wikipedia*. Retrieved December 2, 2011. http://en.wikipedia.org/wiki/Theodosius_I.

Theophilus of Antioch. *Wikipedia*. Retrieved September 14, 2010. http://en.wikipedia.org/wiki/Theophilus_of_ Antioch.

Theotokos. *Wikipedia*. Retrieved March 23, 2012. http:// en.wikipedia.org/wiki/Theotokos.

Thiel, B. *Melito of Sardis*. Retrieved September 18, 2010. http://www.cogwriter.com/melito.htm.

Thurston, H. Easter Controversy. *The Catholic Encyclopedia*. New York: Robert Appleton Company, 1909. Retrieved November 1, 2011. http://www.newadvent.org/cathen/ 05228a.htm.

Timeline of the Book of Acts from the Bible. Retrieved May 24, 2012. http://www.generationword.com/bible_ school_notes/Timeline%20of%20Acts.htm.

Trinity A. *Abiding Peace Lutheran Church—Budd Lake, NJ*. June 19, 2011. Retrieved February 5, 2012. http://www.abidingpeacechurch.org/2011-06-19.pdf.

Wade, R. Justin Martyr: Defender for the Church. *Probe Ministries*, July 17, 2002. Retrieved August 24, 2010. http://www.leaderu.com/orgs/probe/docs/justin.html.

Weisser, T. *Jesus' Name Baptism Through The Centuries*. 1989. Retrieved November 29, 2010. www.geocities. com/robert_upci/jesus_name_baptism_through_the_ centuries_weisse…

Wilhelm, J. The Nicene Creed. *The Catholic Encyclopedia*. New York: Robert Appleton Company, 1911. Retrieved October 26, 2011. http://www.newadvent.org/cathen/ 11049a.htm.

Wommack, A. 1 Corinthians 14:4. *Andrew Wommack Ministries*. Retrieved November 4, 2009. http://www. awmi.net/bible/1co_14_04.

Yeshua (name). *Wikipedia*. Retrieved May 23, 2012. http:// en.wikipedia.org/wiki/Yeshua_%28name%29.

Zeitlin, S. The Great Revolt (66–70 C.E.). *Jewish Virtual Library*. Retrieved May 15, 2010. http://www.jewish virtuallibrary.org/jsource/Judaism/revolt.html.

www.ingramcontent.com/pod-product-compliance
Lightning Source LLC
LaVergne TN
LVHW042249070526
838201LV00089B/87